EMILY NASH

Just A Sharp Scratch

Copyright © 2020 by Emily Nash

All rights reserved. No part of this publication may be reproduced, stored or transmitted in any form or by any means, electronic, mechanical, photocopying, recording, scanning, or otherwise without written permission from the publisher. It is illegal to copy this book, post it to a website, or distribute it by any other means without permission.

First edition

*This book was professionally typeset on Reedsy.
Find out more at reedsy.com*

For My Dad
The bravest and strongest man I know. Thank you for giving me the courage to carry on.

Contents

1	Introduction	1
2	Cough, Temperature and DIB	4
3	Where Did Everyone Go?	9
4	Emily, Something Has Been Brought To My Attention	21
5	Don't Think Anyone Lives There	26
6	The Machines Got To Be Broken	31
7	Bike Vs Uber	34
8	The Press Are Outside Again	39
9	Whatever Happens, Keep Us Together	41
10	Watching Magic Happen	45
11	Bad Neighbours	48
12	Miss, I Think You Should Take A Look!	52
13	The Whistleblower	56
14	Well That's What You Get For Ignoring Me	59
15	Paramedic Humour	63
16	Their Stories	67
17	She has stopped breathing … right?	76
18	Broken Nail	79
19	The Past Can Come Back To Haunt You	80
20	Let's Talk About Mental Health	83
21	"Please let me go to the party mummy"	86
22	Time To Panic	91
23	Your not wasting our time!	95
24	You're gonna need to break the door down	99

25	Sides of domestic abuse	102
26	It's A Girl!	108
27	Please Drive Carefully, His Life Depends On It.	113
28	Always Know How To Get Out Of Dodge.	116
29	Love Thy Neighbour	120
30	Life As We Know It	124
About the Author		126
Also by Emily Nash		127

1

Introduction

I remember very clearly sitting on my bed and starting the first chapter of *Just A Few Bumps*. If someone had told me that I would have published that book and go on to write a second, I would have laughed! But here we are.

I am still working for the London Ambulance Service, and still drinking far too much Red bull. One thing that has changed immensely is my confidence levels. I still get palpitations when certain jobs come down on our screens, and I still get sweaty palms if I see the age of my patient pop up on the screen, and it is below 10. Having confidence mixed with anxiety is a common occurrence in this line of work. Still, I heard something on a podcast a little while ago that put much into perspective, "Why do we fear stress? Stress is good, it means we give a damn." —and I couldn't agree with that statement more. To work in healthcare, you have to give a damn, and to give a damn means welcoming stress into our lives—but it does not have to affect us negatively. Stress can be a tool to strengthen our lives, make us more organised, make us work harder, set targets, achieve goals, and most of all get our lives where we want them to be. I am working on my life every single day. Where do I want to be? What needs to be achieved next, and how can I get there? It is a work in progress. Let's face it, if we got absolutely everything we wanted all at once—where would the fun be in that?

I guess I cannot avoid the giant elephant in the room, otherwise known as Corona Virus. Yes, the global pandemic that has enforced two nationwide lockdowns, cancelled holidays, lost jobs, caused financial struggles, kept families apart and worst of all, taken lives. No one could have predicted how this virus was going to tip our lives upside down. For example, who would have thought that first dates would have to take place over Zoom? Seeing the grandparents would consist of blowing kisses through closed windows, and the queue for Sainsbury's would lap around the car park. The world has gone insane. We now have to wear a mask to walk into a restaurant, but can take it off as soon as we sit down…like I said, insane.

We are now in a world of contactless payments, elbow handshakes, fashionable face masks, video chat, crowd-less arenas, plastic screens, antibacterial sanitizer, and hug-less encounters. In the space of one year, our entire way of living has changed. The way we receive our medical care has changed also. Now my personal protective equipment bag is bulging at the seams, with new protocols being introduced every day. During the height of the pandemic, we had to don a face mask, goggles, double gloves, and an apron for every patient. Now I want you to try and imagine driving to a critically ill patient, and once arriving on the scene having to go into the back of the ambulance and dress in all this kit—before you even step *near* the patient. Not always ideal when someone is choking on the kitchen floor. However, I understand why we need to do this, it is difficult to adjust sometimes.

Don't worry, this book isn't going to be just about the depressing nature that is 2021. I will talk about the funny jobs, the interesting jobs, and the scary jobs, but this book wouldn't be realistic if I didn't talk about the sad jobs and mention how this pandemic has changed the way we practice medicine—in the emergency setting.

As always, to protect the confidentiality of my patients, locations have been removed and any names and ages have been changed, but they are all real. Their emotions, their struggles, their lives. It is all real.

2

Cough, Temperature and DIB

I returned to practice after my months off with PTSD to be greeted with the full force of Covid-19. I had a few days to familiarise myself with the MANY new protocols and procedures that were now involved while dealing with Covid patients, and off I went. What astonished me most was the number of people we were leaving at home, with instructions to call back when their symptoms got worse. Yes, you read that right. We were instructed to take observations from these ill people, but unless they were critically ill, they were to remain at home and isolate and we would basically wait to see if they got worse or started to get better. It soon turned into an operation of repeating the same advice and guidance, taking observations, and being out of the house in less than a few minutes.

Our numbers in the mess room were dropping quickly as colleagues were becoming sick or having to isolate themselves at home. It doesn't help when a lot of paramedics live in shared houses together, so when one has to isolate, you end up losing another five members of staff who are living with them. The number of calls per day was relentless; some calling because family members were seriously ill, some calling because they themselves were struggling to breathe. Others calling because they wanted to be tested for Corona Virus, a service which of course the Ambulance Service does not perform.

With doctor's surgeries being shut, this put a heavy weight on the shoulders of the Ambulances, which I believe we carried with incredible strength and pride. I now drive along the streets of London and see rainbows in windows, and billboards thanking the NHS, and there are donated gifts left at ambulance stations. The kindness and thanks we have received have been overwhelming and at times tear-jerking.

On Thursday my partner Chris and I sat out in our garden readying ourselves for the weekly NHS clap and I got a facetime call from my Mum—she often rang me at this time so we could clap together, but this night she went the extra mile. My mum stood clapping and cheering at the front of her driveway while my dad blared out of the car radio David Bowie's Heroes. I laughed, cried, and cringed, but most of all I told my parents how much I loved them.

I had members of the public leave chocolates and notes on the windows of our truck, I even had a biker pull up to my driver's-side window—while I was driving on blue lights to a job—to blow me a kiss and give me a nod of appreciation. It was definitely a strange time, with the world full of fear of the unknown, yet there was so much love being shared amongst the community.

The contrast of patients was severe, as always, we had the critically ill Covid patients that we were hearing about on the news, and then we had the patients who left us asking why they called in the first place. The first time I saw Covid in its pure unnatural form was with a fit and healthy male in his 50s. He was a contractor by trade and a very active man, no prior health conditions apart from occasionally liking a pint at the weekend. His wife had called us as she was concerned about her partner's breathing. He recently had a positive diagnosis for Covid, and his wife had noticed a change in him. Of course, this gentleman thought his wife was just overreacting and that he would be fine in a couple of days. Well on our arrival I didn't think too differently from this gentleman. He appeared fine to me, his breathing was a bit quicker than we would class as 'normal' however, he was talking in clear sentences and enjoying a nice cup of tea. How bad could he be? My crewmate sat down and started the normal line of questioning, I began checking his vital signs. I started by placing my oxygen saturation probe (sats probe) on his finger, while the device was analyzing I grabbed the tympanic and measured his temperature. He was sitting at a nice 36.8 degrees. Well within normal limits. I looked back to my sats probe and it was reading 80% oxygen and a heart rate of 91 bpm. I pulled it off and tried another finger because the machine must be reading his levels wrong. I have seen many patients with oxygen levels that low but they look 'big sick' and are usually really struggling to breathe, this gentleman, however, was still sitting quite comfortably. The readings still came out the same. I then tested his slow capillary refill, making his low oxygen levels more believable. I continued by lifting his shirt and saw mild mottling to his skin. I then decided enough with the investigations, and let's get this gentleman some oxygen. My crewmate looks rather surprised when I started setting up the oxygen, but after showing them his vital signs they agreed and this gentleman, to the shock of his family, was being blued into the nearest hospital just a few minutes later. Leaving his tea behind sadly. It became very common to see patients breathing relatively well but their oxygen levels being drastically lower than where they should be. This made identifying our 'big sick' patient increasingly difficult. However, one of my more memorable Covid patients could be identified as not sick at all from the moment we walked into the restaurant where he worked. The job came down as: ? Covid, coughing, throat burning 27-year-old male.

As we walked into the restaurant, a young male, who appeared to be one of the waiters, came walking over and identified himself as the patient. He looked well, but a little flushed. We sat at one of the restaurant tables and we started hearing what had happened to this gentleman precipitating him to call an ambulance:

'So, I was in the kitchen and I put the floor cleaner into the bucket.'

'...yes,' I replied.

'Well when I poured in the boiling water, I breathed in a load of steam and it burnt the back of my throat. I couldn't stop coughing and I got worried I caught Covid.'

'Wait, you thought you caught Covid from the steam?' there is a slight pause before his reply.

'Yeah.'

'It doesn't work like that. I can happily say that your cough is probably the result of just breathing in chemically-infused steam. Get some fresh air and you should feel better in no time.'

'Ah, thank you, I was so worried!'

'No problem, glad we could help.' And off we went. He was a sweet guy and we did end up having a giggle about the whole situation but unfortunately, they don't all end up that well. Normally when we go to a lot of 'big sick' patients and we end up blue lighting them to hospital 9 times out of 10 the patient will survive and after a stint in hospital will be back in their homes enjoying life again. For a lot of my 'big sick' Covid patients, this just wasn't the case. A lot didn't come back home.

3

Where Did Everyone Go?

When the government realised the ever-climbing numbers of infected citizens weren't going away on their own, lockdown was brought upon the nation. Businesses, restaurants, trains, pubs, nightclubs, hairdressers, tattoo parlours, you name it—they were shut. London was quiet, and along with it the London Ambulance Service. People became so scared of hospital and ambulances they just stopped calling. On a normal day, we, as crews on an ambulance, were seeing around eight patients on a 12-hour shift. During the lockdown, we were lucky to see three patients. People just stopped calling, but not because people weren't sick, but because people were scared. It got so bad at one point the London Ambulance Service put out a statement (roughly quoting) 'We are still open 24/7—please call us in an emergency.'

There was one major difference I noticed during this time when patients did call. They were 'big sick' because they had either left their symptoms too long in fear of going to the hospital or they tried to treat things at home when their condition couldn't be treated at home. A friend of mine at work once told me about a 'disagreement' (we can call it that) he had with his elderly patient. She did not want to go to the hospital in case she caught Covid despite the fact she was having a major heart attack and probably would not last the night if she stayed at home. We went from being inundated with calls to basically receiving none.

During this time, however, it was actually the break we all needed because after a big job we had time to head back to the station, have a cup of tea, and talk about what had just happened, or sit in silence and digest. Time which is something a lot of healthcare professionals, especially in the emergency setting, simply don't get. We were no longer getting drunken Saturday night punters or bike vs car road traffic collisions; what we were getting a lot of; however, was mental health calls. The Health Foundation actually put out a statement regarding health care workers predicting that depression and PTSD would increase due to this pandemic.

The Mental Health Foundation released findings from a study during this pandemic and found that 45% of the UK population by August 2020 was feeling anxious or worried regarding the pandemic and 10% were feeling suicidal. 15% were feeling hopeless, and 11% stated they felt panicked. Not sure I can agree with these results as I am pretty sure they did not ask every single person in the UK how they felt, (as I don't remember being asked). Still, these are the findings regardless, and I think we can all see now why mental health calls drastically increased during lockdown.

Anyway, do you need a giant organisation or me to tell you why people were scared? Probably not. It was plastered all over our screens daily. It was on the news banners that pinged our phones every five minutes. It was on shop doors and building floors. IT IS EVERYWHERE. People that suffer from mental health problems often keep it all bottled up inside, hidden from the judging eyes of the world, but how can you do that when the whole world is watching your every move? If there is one thing that I can say to relieve the anxiety and stress if you are one of those suffering at the moment, is that you are not alone. The world may be watching right now, but the world is feeling too. Feeling stress, worry, anxiety, fear. The world is also feeling strength and love, please—*please* don't forget that. When it seems that there is complete darkness do not close your eyes, because soon, your eyes will adjust, and the light will filter in.

I talked about my own struggle with mental health in my previous book. I am happy to say that I am doing a lot better. I reached out for help and received counselling for my PTSD and also reached out to a company called Able Futures. It is an organisation that helps you deal with your mental health problems and helps you to return to work. You can find more details on www.able-futures.co.uk. I really recommend them if you are struggling with any mental health problems, and it is affecting you in the workplace.

Balancing on the Edge

Right, enough about the depressing state of our country and back on to the main topic, that is emergency medicine. I am going to talk to you about some of the jobs I went to over the lockdown period. One of which was a mental health call I attended, which in fact turned out to be one big misunderstanding. We were called to a woman in her 40s who, unbeknown to us at the time, was staying at her Mum's house and a lot of the family were also staying there during the lockdown period. She had been struggling with her mental health for the last couple of weeks, and this evening, she decided to reach out to the local mental health crisis number. She had been chatting to the call taker for some time in her room about how she was feeling and how low she had gotten over the last couple of weeks. According to the call taker, the patient had mentioned that she was hanging out of her second-story window and wanted to jump. So, as you can imagine, we were called to her location. The job came down like this.

MH crisis, about to jump out of the window, wants to commit suicide. Gender: F Age: UK

UK = unknown. This job had us worried. We were also informed that police were en route to this address to assist as it was potentially a traumatic job in a public place. Luckily, we all arrived at the same time; unfortunately for this patient her house was directly in front of a busy main road with many onlookers now gawking at the numerous flashing lights outside her residence. We all jumped out of our vehicles quickly and started scanning the windows and the roof but could not see the patient. We searched the area around the house, and thankfully we still could not see the patient. Then I notice a terrified-looking elderly lady peering out of the property's window. I walked up to the window and asked if she could open the door. The whole ordeal of all of us swarming the property had scared the living crap out of everyone inside. Eventually, someone answered the door, and I asked to speak to the patient, the elderly woman was clearly quite confused and started frantically screaming the patient's name, and about five seconds later the patient appeared at the doorway, red-faced and clearly confused. There must have been at least 10 other people standing around in the hallway. We very quickly realised that this patient had called the crisis team in private, and the family actually had no idea of the patient's struggles. We also quickly found out that the patient had no intention of killing herself, she in fact had been asked by the call taker where she was, and the patient responded by saying that she was sitting on her window ledge. So, after the discussion from the patient she then had to go back inside and explain to her whole family why an ambulance and seven police officers were standing outside. I did feel bad for her as she clearly was incredibly embarrassed and really wasn't expecting the response that she got from calling the crisis team.

Neighbours Gone Bad

Another phenomenon we saw rise during lockdown was domestic violence. Families being cooped up together for long periods of time is never a good idea, and in this case, it was neighbours who finally came to blows. We were called to a 16-year-old female that had been cut in the face with a broken piece of glass during an argument with the residents of the flat next door. Police were already on scene and requesting our assistance. When we arrive, the fight had been stopped, and both parties were now inside their homes, talking to the police. We were directed into our patient's address, and thankfully when we arrived, we soon saw that her cuts were superficial, easily treatable and shouldn't leave any scarring. We had a chat about the fight and got their version of events.

According to them, the 'mother' (who turned out not to be the mother) was outside on the phone having a private conversation when the next-door neighbour's daughter came out, and out of nowhere started violently attacking her. This then causes the daughter and the neighbour's mother to come out, and a full-blown fight erupts between the households, finally resulting in the 16-year-old being cut on the face with a broken shard of glass.

I stayed with the patient and took all of her details while my crewmate went outside to talk to the police. The mother to the 16-year-old (which we found out later was actually her drug dealer) asked if she could take her up to the hospital instead of having to go up with us and I replied I would let them know what's happening after I have spoken to the police. Just as I finished talking, my phone went off, I pulled it out and saw my crewmate's icon appear on my screen—he had just sent me a message. It read: 'We don't need to take her in as she is about to be arrested, so when you are done come outside.' *Brilliant,* I thought to myself. I went outside and got information that it was in fact, the patient and the 'mother' that had attacked the other mother and daughter. I saw the door open to the next-door neighbour's house and asked if the people inside needed any medical attention; the police officer gestured for me to go inside and have a look.

When I walked in, I was greeted with pleasantries; however, I was shocked at what I saw. A woman in her 60s sat on the sofa, completely black and blue from bruising to her face. Her left eye was so badly swollen that she could no longer see out of it. The police had called us for a small cut to a young girl's face but had neglected to inform us of the badly beaten woman that was sat just next door. Without giving her much of a say, I told this woman she needed to go to the hospital, and with that, her worried husband practically carried her out of the door to the ambulance. Of course, we cannot take anyone against their will if they have the capacity, and she did finally agree to come; however, I am not too sure she knew what day it was with all the shock of what had just happened. Now we all know there are three sides to every story: the two parties and the truth, but this was the story that we got from the other party. The original patient's 'mother' was outside on the phone f-ing and jeff-ing about the neighbours next door, as they had recently had a new baby welcomed into the home, and the baby's cries were getting a bit much for the neighbours. The daughter came out of patient number two's house and confronted her. This resulted in patient number one coming out and beating up the daughter, and then the rest is history. All one big bloody mess if you ask me, which resulted in three arrests and two trips to the hospital. Neighbours hey!

It Is My Human Right to Be Checked Over

I like to think of myself as a calm, patient individual, but everyone has their limits. There have been times where I have been pushed to boiling point, and it has happened to me now twice in the job where professionalism goes out the window. Both times in fact were hoax cardiac arrests. The occasion I'm about to describe happened at the height of the lockdown when death was on the rise. My crewmate and I had managed to get a break (which does not always happen!) However, towards the end of your break, you can be taken off it for a CAT 1 job, i.e., life-threatening conditions where death could be imminent. So, on this night shift, 15 minutes before the end of our break our radio buzzes, and we both know it is a CAT 1 job. I take a quick look at the screen and see **'cardiac arrest - 27 yr/M'**. Broken down, this means a 27-year-old male has died, and we were only one mile away from the patient.

'Shit, it's a cardiac arrest,' I say as I read the screen and we both jump up off the sofas and run to the truck and hit the blue lights. Now, with our new pandemic protocols of PPE (personal protective equipment), we must wear full kit to any cardiac arrest due to the close proximity we have to patient airways during a resuscitation. So, my crewmate and I jump in the back of the truck and begin the horrendous task of trying to put a full jumpsuit on over our uniform, double gloves, full face face-masks, all as quickly as possible. Now you can imagine at this point our adrenaline is high, the sweat build-up is intense, and so is the stress level. What is making things worse is the radio in the main cab keeps buzzing, meaning someone is trying to get hold of us. So, as graceful as always, with one leg caught in my suit, I lunge through into the cab and grab the receiver.

'X103' (call sign)

'X103, yes hi, sorry about this guys, but police are en route and can you wait for their arrival, we had a similar call to this five days ago, and the patient threatened the crew.'

'Oh, really? Okay, we will wait for the police.'

The police never take long to reach us on a job like this, but it still adds even more of a delay, and if the patient is indeed in cardiac arrest, every minute counts. 9 in 10 people will not survive an out-of-hospital cardiac arrest. This is predominantly due to ineffective CPR or a delay in carrying out CPR and providing good ventilation. I do strongly believe that First Aid should be taught in school as a core subject along with Math, English and Science. Most 16-year-olds can tell me who won the Battle of Hastings in 1066 but not how to help someone that is choking or suffering from a bad allergic reaction. These kids should be taught how to place someone in the recovery position and how to perform good quality CPR. *Obviously not at the same time.*

It is a horrific thought, I know, that a child might ever need to perform these skills, but medical emergencies happen every day. Unfortunately, they don't wait until after the watershed. While you're reading this book, please ask yourself, if someone was dying before your very eyes and they stopped breathing, would you know what to do? If not, I strongly suggest you check out some videos online or some training courses. Better to know it and not need it, than to need it and not know it.

Back to our young gentleman who is, according to his 999 calls, in cardiac arrest. The police have arrived on the scene, and we are high tailing our way up the three flights of stairs to his flat. The door, thankfully, is open, so we do not need to waste more time in smashing the door down. The police enter first calling out the gentleman's name and frantically searching rooms hoping we are going to find him alive and well. Finally, we find him. He is lying on the living room floor, a pillow under his head and an empty pill bottle lying by his hand. However, despite the typical overdose movie scene appearance, something isn't feeling right to me and my crewmate. The patient's phone is also held in his other hand. The other thing that seems off is that it is quite obvious to us that this gentleman is holding his breath. After seeing a few dead people, you come to realise instantly if someone is dead or not. The guy was not dead. So, while my crewmate did the usual 'Sir, sir, can you hear me?' I took it upon myself to pick up his phone. My thinking was that I could look at his call list to see if he had rung 999 because let's face it, you can't call in your own cardiac arrest, and no one else was in the property. Well, I have to say I have never seen someone jump up so quickly in all my life—this guy reached out and snatched the phone out of my hand.

'That's mine. You can't have my phone.'

'Wow, that got you up didn't it, Sir.' I was trying my best to sound serious, but of course, I was sarcastic.

'Fuck off,' was his reply.

'Sir, what's going on? we have been called to this address for a cardiac arrest?'

'I don't know what's happened. I was unconscious!'

'Well, you weren't unconscious when we got here? Who called the ambulance?'

'I don't fucking know, probably a friend! Why are the fucking pigs here!?'

'Well sir, they're here because a call for a cardiac arrest came in for this address just a few days ago, and apparently you threatened staff, so they are here for our safety and to make sure you are okay.'

'Well, I don't fucking want them here, so get the fuck out.'

'OK can you stop swearing, there really isn't any need for it. We need to know what's been going on, and while you're reacting like this, they are not going to leave. So, who is this friend and where did he go, because there wasn't anyone here when we arrived apart from yourself.'

'I don't know he must have left.'

'So, your friend thought you were dead, called an ambulance and then just left? Pretty strange behaviour, isn't it?'

'Are you going to check me over or what?! Your fucking neglecting me, I've taken an overdose you stupid bitch!' With this, my crewmate picks up the said bottle of pills and reads the label out loud.

'They're vitamin C tablets.'

'Yeah so?!'

'Well, apart from some funny coloured urine, I think you are going to be fine.'

'You need to check my blood pressure and heart rate. I know how this works—you need to check me over!'

'Okay, calm down!'

I begin to attach our equipment to the patient while my

crewmate continues to ask more questions. However, it seems asking questions is just antagonising the patient more, and out of nowhere his demeanour changes.

'See you, you little bitch, I've got a nice machete that would love to meet you.'

'What did you just say?' I interrupt as he stares viciously at my crewmate.

'And a nice gun to finish it off,' he turns to me. With that, I start ripping off the equipment and packing up our kit. My crewmate, being the professional one at this moment, is keeping her cool and trying to defuse the situation.

'What are you doing? It's my human right to be medically checked over!' he screams at me.

'And it is also my right to walk out if you are threatening my crewmate or myself, so we are leaving!'

'You can't leave you fucking slut!'

'Watch me. Let's go.' The hail of abuse continued as we walked off the property.

'I'm going to find your Mum and rape her and fuck her titties,' echoed down the hallway as we got into the stairwell.

So, the moral of that job is that hoax calls do happen, and that patient was just a nasty piece of work. But half an hour later after finishing some paperwork and calming down we were off and ready for another job.

I think we will all remember the lockdown for many years to come—for many different reasons. For me, I will always remember the generosity of others in such dark negative times. With businesses being shut down and families losing money on a daily basis, the nation still looked out for one another. We as the NHS were receiving donations on a daily basis—food, drinks, clothes, cosmetics, you name it, and all just to say thank you. It was unbelievably heart-warming and selfless and I would like to take this opportunity to say a big Thank You. Not just for the NHS, but to all the families that looked after others when they did not have to. To the communities that made meals and delivered them to the shielded residents. To those that did shopping for others, for those that picked up medication for the elderly so they did not have to. I said in my last book that the world could be a kinder place and I truly believe we saw many heroic acts of humanity during the year 2020. Obviously not including my last patient.

4

Emily, Something Has Been Brought To My Attention

One of our main responsibilities as paramedics is to be aware of vulnerable adults and children and to look out for children and adults that need safeguarding. For this chapter, I will keep the subject to children.

Now with children, some of the things clinicians in the pre-hospital setting would look out for are: dirty clothes, malnourishment, overly quiet or overly attentive with strangers, strange cuts or bruises, use of drugs in the house, a dirty home, lack of appropriate facilities for children i.e., a bed or the right size nappies, a working bath or shower. Now I am no saint and I am fully aware of how easy it can be sometimes to judge others, especially when it comes to parenting. I'm not going to lie to you, I myself have been to some jobs and looked on in horror at how some children live, but I have also learned over time that sometimes the parents are in a tough situation and they really are just trying their best.

However, there have been times when I have seen the parents in lovely decorated bedrooms with a comfy double bed, yet their child is sleeping on a mattress on the floor. I have also seen parents shouting at their child: 'George, get off the fucking table,' and proceed to smack then round the back of the ear. Then carry on talking to me with sweetness and light. I am under no illusion that raising children is an easy task and I salute the single parents of the world. Now you would think spotting a neglected and hurt child is easy, we have all seen the child abuse cases such as 'Baby P' and we want to scream at the TV screen 'How did they not stop this, how did they not spot it!' but I am holding my hands up now and telling you I missed one. And it has stuck with me.

It is around 11pm and we get a job come down our screen, it is a referral from 111, and the job is about four hours old. It is for a one-year-old that has fallen out of his carrier and sustained a bump to his head. We pop on the blue lights and start making our way to the address. When we arrive, we are met by a lovely young man that shows us up to the flat. When we walk in, we are greeted by a very smiley and giggly one-year-old. Mum and baby are both in the living room.

'Hello, there little one, what happened to you, aye?' I crouch down and squeeze his little hand in mine. The baby then produces the most heart-warming smile in my direction.

'He likes the ladies,' said the Mum.

'Oh, does he now? Little heart breaker already!'

'Hello Mum, what's happened today then?' I turn my gaze now to Mum and Dad.

'So, my partner was bringing 'baby' (I will call the patient baby for confidentiality) out of the car in his car seat/carrier and as he came in the handle broke and he rolled out and bumped his head on the floor.' I looked at 'baby' and there to the right of his temple was a minor graze and small bump.

'Ok, did he cry instantly after the fall?'

'Yeah, but I gave him a cuddle and he stopped pretty quickly afterwards.'

'OK, so he never became lethargic or was rolling his eyes back, didn't lose consciousness, any vomiting?' I asked

'No, he was fine, a little while later he had some milk.'

'Has he been filling his nappies as normal?'

'Yeah.'

'Ok, so you called 111 just for advice?'

'Yeah, I just wanted to know what to look out for but he has been fine since, he's had a bath, had a couple of feeds and he just woke up from a nap about an hour ago.'

'Ok, this is great. Well, it sounds like it's just a small bump to the head, but just to be on the safe side we'll pop him up to A&E to get checked out properly.'

'Oh, do we have to go? It's just I've got him all ready for bed and I really think he's fine.'

'To be honest, I don't disagree with you, he *is* probably fine, but our policy is to take anyone under the age of two to the hospital because children can quickly decline, but that is a worst-case scenario.'

'I understand, well can we see how he goes and if things change, we can take him up to hospital ourselves? My partner has a car.' I hesitate here not knowing what's best to do.

'Well, we will need to refer him to his GP if he was to stay at home—it's nearly midnight and your GP is not open so I will have to speak to an on-call GP at 111 and they can do a call-back to yourselves and inform your GP in the morning.'

'I have already spoken to my GP, they're aware and I have an appointment first thing in the morning.'

'Oh brilliant!'

'I rang 111 first, then after that spoke to the GP.'

'And the GP was happy to see you in the morning?' I ask.

'Yeah, it's from 9am.'

'I know it's not your job but what do you recommend we do about this carrier,' the Dad asks from behind me.

'Well definitely don't use it again, I'd suggest getting in contact with the company you brought it from and requesting a new one,' I have a look at the carrier and it is indeed broken.

I turned to my crewmate and we were both on the same page as far as this job was concerned. The baby's vital signs were all normal, he was feeding, sleeping and his nappies were fine, it was now five-hours since the head bump and there were no red-flag signs. The family were proactive in his care and had spoken to three health care professionals now regarding their child and had a GP appointment booked for the morning. We deemed the child safe to stay at home, we left a copy of our paperwork and a lot of advice on what to look out for, going forward. We said our goodbyes and left the scene.

Now jump forward a month and I get an email from my manager to come in and have a chat, (never a good sign). We meet and it goes something like this:

'Hi Emily, how are you?'

'I'm good thanks, what's up?'

'Well, I received an email today about one of your jobs and I need your statement on it.'

'Statement?' My manager then goes on to describe the job to me and I recognise pretty quickly that it is the 'baby' with the head bump.

'Why didn't you refer to a GP if they didn't want to go to the hospital?' my manager asks. I go on to explain the job in detail and why we did what we did.

'What's this all about?' I ask.

'Well, it has come to our attention that this child has a safeguarding concern for abuse and it is currently under investigation.' My heart sinks.

'Is the child OK?' I ask, eyes wide.

'I believe so, there was another incident and the child had to go to the hospital and so your paperwork was flagged. It appears there has been a number of similar 'accidents' and the couple's previous child has been taken away to child protection services.

'So, you're telling me the parents probably hit him or caused his injury on purpose?'

'Well, we don't know, that's why an investigation is happening. So, I just need your full statement and I have a few questions about the scene and the carrier.'

We spend about an hour going over the job and what I and my crewmate had seen and said, my statement was sent off to the investigators.

I still don't know to this day if it was an accident like the parents had told me or if the injury had occurred on purpose. I don't know if that child is still in the care of his parents or has been taken away like his sibling. It was a very big wake up call for me and I learned that all children need to be safeguarded in some way, whether it is chatting to the GP, taking them to the hospital or referring them to a safeguarding team, because something so innocent can be like a wolf in sheep's clothing.

5

Don't Think Anyone Lives There

Warning alert for this chapter: it's sad and somewhat gruesome.

I am back on relief at this point and that means you generally work with someone different each shift. I was crewed up with this lovely woman, and so far we were having a decent shift. The normal run of the mill jobs such as chest pain, chronic illness and the occasional GP referral. We decided to take a break and were sitting at the station enjoying a cup of tea. A few minutes before the end of our break we heard a general broadcast over the radio. A general broadcast (GB) is when the allocator in the control centre has a back-up list of jobs, and he or she reads them out, to see if anyone is near the job and available so that they can 'green' up for them (take the job).

A few jobs were described over the radio but one that stuck out to myself and my crewmate was just around the corner and sounded rather odd. It was a welfare call for an address that was reported to have maggots coming out of the property. This means two things, one, the house is extremely dirty (which I'd rather not go to), or two, the patient is dead and has been for some time. Either way, this job wasn't going to be a pleasant one.

The moment our break finished we heard the familiar sound of our radio's buzzing, meaning we had a job sent down to us and it was this job regarding the maggots. Control buzzed us shortly afterwards to inform us that police were also on their way to this job in case we needed to force entry.

The police were already on scene when we got there a few minutes later and we could see them standing on the first-floor balcony trying to break the door down. They obviously had enough concern for this patient's welfare to start breaking down the door before our arrival as generally, they would wait for us. By the time we had got our kit and began walking to the main entrance doors, a policewoman called down to us stating we wouldn't need all our kit. I looked at my colleague, slightly confused, and wondered if this meant that there was no one home.

'Is the place empty?' we called out to the officers on the balcony.

'Come and take a look.' is all they replied. So, we put our kit back and made our way into the block of flats. We took the stairs and pushed the doors that lead to the first-floor flats. People talk about the smell of death and how it cannot be confused with any other smell. That it ingrains in your nose hairs and lingers on your clothes and in the pores of your skin. Well, all these statements are true. The smell hit me hard in the face and it took a lot for me to remain professional and not to gag. We met the officer standing at the door and I noticed that they hadn't been able to break the door open fully. The bottom left-hand corner of the door had been kicked in, revealing a small window into the flat which was about 50cm x 50cm. I crouched down and tried to peer in but it was too dark inside and the smell was keeping me back.

'Can you see the body?' I asked the officer as I stood up again. The police officer looked at me for a second and then got her torch out, and with a click she shone the light down to the break in the door.

'Oh fuck!' I shrieked as the light revealed a decaying skull that lay on the floor just by the door. I had been no more than a foot away but could not see it at first due to the bone of the skull which had turned black. It is a part of the process of decay. The rest of the patient's body was lying behind the door, meaning kicking the door down was definitely not an option now. It took a few more seconds for my crewmate to notice and she yelped out also. As you can imagine, we started getting an audience of neighbours wanting to know what was going on.

'Excuse me,' I asked as I approached the woman that lived next door. 'Do you the gentleman's name that lives here?'

'I didn't think anyone lived there. I've never seen them before.'

'Just out of interest how long has this smell been here?' I had to ask her as there is no way this smell would have gone unnoticed.

'Oh about a month or so, the council are trying to sort the water out I think.'

'Hm, it's not the pipes causing the smell.' I finished before I turned back to my colleague. My crewmate went back down to the truck to call his GP after the police had obtained the details of who lived in the property. She informed them he has passed away and gained a bit of information regarding the patient. From the phone call, we found out that this gentleman was 35 years old and suffered from Type 1 Diabetes. Likely cause of death was hypoglycaemia. He had no next of kin and no family history. No one had reported him missing for over two months, which is what we had estimated from the state of his decay. It broke my heart, to say the least, that no one knew he wasn't with us anymore. He left this world in the most horrific way. With no one by his side and no one to think of him.

I went home to my partner that night and we raised a glass in memory of 'John' just so someone would toast his life. John may have liked the solitude, he may have chosen to live that way, he also might have been extremely lonely. All I can hope is that he was happy in his life. All I can say is smile at your neighbours, say good morning, smile at the man or woman that walks past you in the street, it may mean nothing to someone but it also might mean the world to them and make their day. Have you ever been caught at the bus stop by an elderly man or woman who keeps chatting to you? To me all that tells me is—hey I haven't spoken to anyone in ages and I just want a conversation with somebody. So, if you've got a spare five minutes, talk away. Ask them about their day, tell them about your day! I'm sure they will appreciate it.

Side-note: If the person appears strange and your gut feeling is telling you not to talk to them then listen to your gut and not necessarily me!

On my last shift, I was sitting in the truck while my colleague was on the phone to the GP when I got a knock on the driver's side window. I drew the window down and this gentleman was standing there, around 40-years-old. He was standing there smiling uncontrollably with a Hogwart's scarf around his neck and a box of Lego that made Ron Weasley's blue car. He just wanted to show me his new Lego that he had just bought. It was quite clear that this gentleman had learning difficulties. I sat there and had a 20-minute conversation about Harry Potter, and who our favourite characters were, and after our chat he walked off again waving enthusiastically at 'his new friends'. Simple things.

6

The Machines Got To Be Broken

We are in the second wave of the pandemic. The new strain has been unleashed across the media and the infection rates are on the rise. Nearly every job we were going to was Covid-related. We had just begun our shift and we got our first call of the day. It was for a ? hypo. This means the patient suffers from diabetes and the main concern is that the patient's sugar levels have dropped dangerously low which can cause confusion, unusual behaviour, slurred speech, seizures, passing out, blurred vision and more. If the patient's sugar levels are extremely low then we can give them medication to quickly boost them back up. I have found that patients with diabetes usually suffer serious hypos because they have mixed up their medication and given themself often double doses of insulin.

On this particular shift, I was working with a fairly new member of staff, so before we arrived on the scene, I ran through a few scenarios of what we could do for this patient—not knowing at the time that all of it would be wasted, as this patient was not suffering from a hypo like the family suspected.

When we arrived, we were directed to a gentleman lying on the bed. He was slightly pale and acting strange. Despite the language barrier, it was quite clear that he was confused. We checked his sugar levels first and they were high but not dangerously so. So, we move on and try to find out why this gentleman is confused and unable to hold his own body weight up. I attach the equipment to him while my colleague tries her best to get a history (there was a language barrier). This is when I start to frown at the machine. His heart rate is showing at 120bpm, his oxygen levels are showing 45%. Now, the lowest oxygen levels I've ever seen are 63% and that was with life-threatening asthma. The patient looked extremely sick and his skin was completely cyanosed (turning blue). The gentleman looked out. He wasn't struggling to breathe and despite his confusion could talk in full sentences.

'The machine must be playing up,' I say while getting my oxygen saturation probe out and taking another reading. Again, it shows 45%. I'm beginning to sweat a little now. I decided to test his capillary refill. This means squeezing the nail bed of a finger and counting how long it takes for the skin to return to its normal colour. Normal perfusion should take less than two seconds, after performing this test on our patient I count to 7. Not good.

'Time to go!' I bark and realising this patient has been off oxygen for too long already we quickly flush him with as much oxygen as we had. His family start panicking and asking why we have to take him to the hospital.

'Has he had a fever or been coughing lately?' I ask as we're trying to get him onto our chair.

'Covid?' One of the family members asks. 'Yes, he has Covid,' she continues. I feel my blood boiling inside because I wish they had said that from the start and also because by this point there were about seven people standing around in the flat and I can take a pretty good guess they all don't live in this two-bed property.

We're out the door in no time and down to the truck, his oxygen levels never go above 85% and he is blued into the nearest hospital. I cannot say for sure but I imagine he was taken to ITU. (Intensive Care Unit)

7

Bike Vs Uber

"If we remembered every day that we could lose someone at any moment, we would love them more fiercely and freely, and without fear—not because there is nothing to lose but because everything can always be lost."—Unknown author.

There are a few things I've learnt about myself while doing this job, and one of them is my ability to grieve with others. The sight of death is sad for me but it's the grief of others that I feel the most. In this line of work, sometimes you need to be able to detach yourself from the person you are treating and see it as a job. It is often cold and it is something I struggle with a lot. I have always managed to keep myself together during these hard jobs but *boy,* it has been really difficult at times.

This particular job will stick with me for many reasons; one being how fragile and short life can be; another for how cold and inconsiderate bystanders can be, and lastly for the pure horrific emotion that is grief.

We had been called to a RTC (road traffic collision) involving a motorbike and a car. Our patient was reportedly lying on the ground still, not moving and '?breathing'. Usually any RTC we attend in London is fairly low impact and nine times out of ten, there is minimal injury. This is due to the dense traffic and low-speed zones. However, serious accidents can happen and this is what happened tonight. We arrive on the scene and our view of the accident is blocked by police cars parked across the street. I am driving the ambulance at this point so I hanker up the brakes and head to the back of the ambulance to grab the necessary equipment. Trauma jobs can sometimes need nothing more than a plaster, but sometimes they can be complex jobs needing an array of equipment and clinical skills, so it's best to be cautious when approaching these kinds of jobs.

Before I had a chance to grab the oxygen bag my crewmate jumped back onto the ambulance and the following events proceeded like this:

'He's arrested!' said my crewmate.

'Oh crap!' I jump out and see the police officer on scene performing CPR on this gentleman in the road.

'Okay, I'll grab the bags.' We grabbed what we needed and ran. A paramedic in a rapid response car has arrived and is trying to ventilate the patient but is clearly struggling from my first glance.

'What needs to be done?' I call out to the other medic on scene.

'Hi, OK I'm on the airway, can you gain access?'

'Yep, on it.' 'Gaining access' means gaining access into a vein so we can give medication to help in the resuscitation process. It is vital during an arrest that we gain IV access, especially in traumatic arrest as it is often that multiple drugs will need to be given along with possible blood and fluids. My crewmate is trying to help also with this patient's airway—ventilation is key in preserving the brain's normal function, as without it the brain is being starved of oxygen. This gentleman's airway, however, was overflowing with blood.

This was my second time, ever, of gaining IO access (intraosseous access). This is where we drill into the proximal tibia or the humeral head, the drill reaches into the bone marrow and we are able to pump drugs straight into there. Often in cardiac arrest, it is hard to maintain vein access, so this is the preferred route. So, as you can imagine it is an odd feeling drilling into someone's legs or shoulder, but it has to be done, so you suck it up and get it done. Police are still performing CPR. My colleagues are still struggling with this gentleman's airway and I was just about to start giving drugs when HEMS doctors arrive on the scene. Do you remember me telling you about the trauma doctors, well if not, that is these guys (HEMS).

'Okay guys, what have we got so far?' asks the lead doctor on the scene. This is where the lead paramedic, generally the first medic on scene hands over to the doctors regarding what has happened right up to this point. It goes like this:

'Ok so our patient is the motorcyclist, he had a head-on collision with the car behind us, he has gone over the handlebars and landed here in the centre of the junction. Bystanders removed his helmet and found the patient unresponsive and not breathing. Police arrive seven minutes later and CPR commenced. We managed to get effective ventilations roughly 15 minutes from when the patient stopped breathing. We have reduced air entry in the lung and suspecting there is a vast amount of blood in his lungs. We have gained IO access in the left proximal tibia and we are just about to give one dose of adrenaline. He has been in a non-shockable rhythm throughout (meaning we are not shocking his heart at this point). Injuries: we are suspecting a broken scapula, clavicle, and humerus on the right-hand side concaved rib cage, and a broken pelvis.'

'Ok, thank you, we are going to open his chest,' replied the doctor. This poor man has probably broken a lot more but this was all we could clearly tell at this point. Regardless of broken bones, the gentleman was dead and we had to do everything we could to bring him back to life. The HEMS doctors cut open a small section in-between his ribs, the aim is to allow whatever is inside the lungs to be removed, i.e. blood. I was watching intently at this point, and I saw the expression change in the doctor's face as blood began to pour out from this gentleman's chest. I didn't have to be a doctor to know what his expression meant. This gentleman was dead and there was nothing we could do for him now. His heart had been torn and the damage was beyond repair.

I don't believe I can describe with justice the adrenaline you feel when you go to a big job such as this and the huge comedown you feel just after the doctor tells you, 'Okay let's stop there, time of death 01:32am.' At 01:31am. there is hope and then at 01:32am., it is done.

I started to collect rubbish and kit from the street when an Incident Response Officer (IRO) came up to me, 'Leave it all where it was Emily, this is deemed a crime scene now.' It took me by surprise because the whole time I never looked at the situation as a crime that had just taken place, but after I looked around at the chaos that had unfolded here I realise that was *exactly* what it was. The car had driven through a red light, probably in a rush to be somewhere and probably imagining they could just make the lights; instead, this caused a man of

35 years to die. The driver of the car was sat in a police car just around the corner. I was asked by a police officer to make sure the driver was okay before they took him to the police station.

'Hello Sir, my name's Emily, you were the driver of the car?'

'Yes Miss,'

'Okay, how are you feeling? Do you have any injuries?'

'No, I think I'm OK just a bit shaken up. How is the other guy, is he responding yet?'

'Erm, we… we're seeing to him.' The police officer had neglected to tell me that he was unaware that our patient was dead. All the guy who was driving the car had to do was step two paces to the right and he would have seen the body lying in the street. Safe to say I just made a quick assessment of the gentleman from the car and got myself out of that situation.

We went back to our vehicles and began writing up our paperwork. Halfway through I decided I needed to get some fresh air and walked down the street to call my partner, when I saw a man standing outside his house just a few doors down from where our patient lay in the street. He had his phone in his hand taking photos and recording video. Rage bubbled up inside of me and I began marching in his direction—luckily for him and myself a police officer got there first and told him what for. There was just no shame—he seemed annoyed that the police officer had approached him and told him to put his phone away and delete the images.

I went back to my phone and continued to Chris (my partner), halfway through my conversation with him was when I heard a wail like nothing I've ever heard before. I walked back around the corner to where the accident was and saw a man and a woman hunched in a ball by the police tape, just screaming. It was the patient's wife and his best friend.

8

The Press Are Outside Again

The peak of the second wave of Covid has hit the UK and the NHS is completely snowed under with patients. The ambulance service are holding calls for hours and we are doing everything we can to reach everyone and triage them appropriately. One particular night we transported our patient to the hospital, and when we arrived, we were told there were no beds available and they were doing everything they could to make space for us. So, we were waiting. We waited with our patient on the ambulance for five hours. Now people can comment saying that it's outrageous that we had to wait that long but what I will say to those people is that I saw how hard the staff worked that night in this particular hospital. The main triage nurse was running around the A&E bays trying to organise an array of patients, alarms were buzzing left, right and centre, there were triage doctors running around the ambulance bays coming into the ambulance to take blood and provide care. My patient was quite poorly but he never moaned once, all he would say is 'Thank you'. The hospital staff and the ambulance crews worked together to get all the patients seen as quickly as possible. I myself left for home five hours later than I should have, but you know what, we are in the midst of a pandemic, so it is what it is. I can say from first-hand experience that that night was one of the busiest nights in London for medical staff and the hospital staff worked so hard and were amazing!

The next morning it was splashed about the press that this hospital was giving terrible care to its patients and that the staff were poor.

DON'T BELIEVE EVERYTHING YOU READ IN THE PRESS.

9

Whatever Happens, Keep Us Together

During the height of Covid, we had to make some tough decisions, some of those were whether to take a person into hospital or try to treat them in the community via their GP with things such as home oxygen equipment.

Sometimes we managed this quite successfully and other times we didn't and we had no choice to take them into the hospital. You would think, well why wouldn't you take sick people into hospital, well the answer is: the hospitals were running out of beds. The hospitals had to divide the wards between Covid patients and non-Covid patients which restricted the number of spaces that were available in the hospitals. The other reason for this was because families weren't permitted to visit their family members once they were in the hospital. As you can imagine this was extremely difficult for the families and also for the patients that were scared and just wanted their husbands, wives, or anyone close to them by their side.

I do not know what each hospital's guidelines were on this

but I do know there was a time where we weren't letting family members come with us to the hospital at all. The only exceptions were if the patient needed a translator or the patient was vulnerable and needed a career or legal guardian with them, i.e., children or elderly dementia patients. This was heartbreaking, telling family members that they couldn't come along with us and call the hospital's main switchboard to find out the progress of a loved one. I, as a paramedic for the NHS, and seeing first-hand what the virus was doing to our country, would have struggled to not hide in a duffle bag and smuggle myself into a hospital if it was my partner or parents. So, I completely understood people's frustration and heartache. There was a particular job that stuck with me regarding this matter and damn near broke my heart. I would be lying to you if I said I didn't shed a tear once I got home from work.

It was a day shift and we were called to an elderly couple's house, the call came back as a backup, as there was already an ambulance on scene, and they were requesting our assistance. We got a general idea of the call and that it was 'difficulty in breathing'. When we are asked to assist other ambulances it can be for many reasons, one of which might be that there isn't a paramedic on the first ambulance and they need a paramedic to perform a clinical skill such as giving fluids or pain relief. Another could be that getting the patient out of the property is proving difficult and they need an extra pair of hands.

It was only when we arrived that we found out why we were called. The first ambulance was called for an elderly woman who had woken up short of breath. Upon their arrival, they were told the women had tested positive for Covid and after assessing her vital signs they found out her oxygen levels were low and her respiratory rate was high. She needed to go to the hospital for treatment. They decided to check the vital signs of the husband who had been isolating with his wife, who had also tested positive for Covid. His oxygen levels were also low. This is when they called through for a second ambulance to assist and treat the husband. We were told all of this on our arrival and at the same time, three women arrived stating they were the patient's daughters and wanted to see how they were doing. Before we could say anything they were inside the house and comforting their parents.

We reached the husband who was roughly 90-years-old and appeared extremely frail. His breathing was extremely affected by Covid. He has short shallow breaths and his oxygen levels were low. We provided him with oxygen and began the extraction process. Both of our patients were going to be blue-lighted into the hospital as critical patients needing urgent treatment.

While we were en route to the hospital the oxygen we had been giving the husband perked him up enough that he was able to speak to me. He was trying to talk to me with the O2 mask over his mouth but I couldn't make out what he was saying so I undid my belt and lifted the mask so I could hear what he was saying.

"Where is my wife?" he asked.

"She is in the other ambulance—she is going to the same hospital as you are."

"Is she OK?"

"She is quite poorly but so are you, so we are going to take care of both of you."

This is when he starts welling up. Balls of tears pool in his eyes and his lip begins to tremble.

"What's the matter?" I ask, my heart was breaking.

"I'm not ready to die." His words nearly break me and it takes a lot of strength not to cry with him. What do you say to someone whose chances of survival are slim yet they are staring you in the face, stating they're not ready to leave this world. I have no words but before I realise what I am doing, I'm leaning over the trolley bed and hugging him. I broke so many rules and protocols but deep down I know if that was my Dad, I would have done the exact same thing and to this day I don't regret it despite people's criticisms. He started mumbling something else and I got myself together enough to ask him to repeat himself.

'What did you say?'

'Can I be with my wife at the hospital?'

'I'll do what I can,' I reply as I don't want to make promises that essentially I have no control over.

We arrive at the hospital shortly after the first ambulance, and after handing the story over to the doctor I pull him aside and inform him that the other elderly woman that was brought in was his wife and the patient asked if they could be put together in the same room. The doctor immediately transferred the husband and wife into the same room.

They got to be together right up to the end. They both died.

10

Watching Magic Happen

In my first book, I wrote that medicine could be like magic, and it is wonderful to watch. There is nothing better than helping a patient to the point where they are no longer unwell and safe to stay at home.

We were on a night shift and got called to a patient suffering from hypoglycaemia. Their sugar levels had reached a dangerous level, and they needed immediate medical attention. This gentleman had Type 1 diabetes, and his partner had called after being woken up in the middle of the night by this man having a seizure in the bed next to him. We arrived on the scene shortly after and found the patient sitting on the bed, sweating profusely and in a daze. We tried to ask the patient questions, but he was bewildered and barely looking at us. His sugar levels were sitting a 1.3. Anything under 4 we would start treating with glucose so they were very low. I put a cannula into his arm and started giving him glucose straight into his vein. This is where the magic happens, just as I'm finishing putting the last ml into his bloodstream, the patient looks down at me and says:

'Wow, I feel better.' Everyone bursts out laughing as moments before he was staring blankly at a wall not reacting to anyone, and now he was smiling down at me, slightly confused I might add. 'When did you guys get here?' he asks.

'You don't remember us walking in?' I reply.

'Nope.'

His partner proceeds to shed a few tears with relief and they hug. We left them in the company of each other and our patient munching on a bag of sweeties.

Another story that always makes me smile is a call for an 87-year-old man. The daughter and wife were on scene and they believe this gentleman was having a stroke. As you can imagine the family was upset when we arrived. I did notice that the wife, who was at least 85 years old herself was marching around the flat gathering bits and putting them in a bag for her husband to go to the hospital with. Clearly flustered and not thinking straight. The daughter started telling us what had happened and explained that her Dad was found by his wife around 30 minutes ago and he was unresponsive on the sofa. He has urinated himself and opened his bowels. His eyes were open, but rolling back in his head. He had no strength in his body and could not hold himself up on the sofa. I and my crewmate quickly performed a fast test and he was showing signs of a stroke. With his other vital signs OK we decided to get him onto a carry chair and get him down to the truck ASAP. Strokes can be caused by a clot in the brain or a bleed on the brain, both are time-critical emergencies so this is where we get moving. Just before we pick the gentleman up off the sofa my colleague asks what his medical history is. The daughter replies, listing various aliments but finishes with diabetes. My crewmate and I stop in unison and stare at each other, both thinking the same thing.

'I'm going to check his sugar levels quick,' I say quickly jumping to our kit bag.

'Yeah, good idea.' Within 30 seconds we get a result that reads 1.3. This is very low and tells us straight away why our patient is in the state he is. He is having a hypoglycaemic episode. Immediately our plans have changed and I am opening up our medications bag and pulling out a vial of glucose. My crewmate injects it into his arm and we sit back and wait, both staring eagerly. The daughter and wife stop as well and wait. We explain what we think is happening and the daughter explains that he has never had a hypo before. His diabetes is normal, very well managed. It only took a few minutes and suddenly the gentleman lifts his head, turns to his wife and a giant smile spreads across his face and says two beautiful words. 'Hello, darling.'

His wife falls to her knees and begins sobbing. Relief pours from her as she realises her husband is going to be OK. They share a sweet hug and our job here is done.

I love my job.

11

Bad Neighbours

You've all heard of the expression, 'nightmare neighbour' well this neighbour should win the award.

We were called to a young woman who had been assaulted and was reportedly bleeding heavily from a head wound. Head wounds can be scary injuries to deal with. It is easy for a head injury to result in internal bleeding, which leads the brain to swell, causing a brain injury. So, with the details of this job coming down to us, we were on high alert that this patient could be severely unwell.

We arrived at a tower block and were greeted by police who were arriving at the same time as us. We made our way up the tower block with all the equipment we might need as we were too far away from the truck to run back for stuff. When we arrived, a young woman answered the door to her flat and the extent of her injuries could be seen immediately. Her right eye was completely swollen and a rather large laceration hung over her right eyebrow. Blood ran down her face and down her neck. We quickly slowed the bleeding from her injury, then found a huge lump to the back of her head that had also split and was actively bleeding.

'What happened?!' I asked as I grabbed for another bandage.

'I just answered the door and he came at me,' she replied in between sobs.

'Wait, start from the beginning.' said the police officer standing behind me.

'I was playing music and cleaning my living room, then I started hearing this banging noise coming from the floor. I gathered my downstairs neighbour was banging on the ceiling but I didn't know why because I wasn't making much noise and my music wasn't that loud. The next thing I know he was banging on my front door, I opened it and got hit in the face several times with a hammer. He was just shouting and swinging the hammer. I thought I was going to die. I managed to shut the door and he just kept smashing my door with the hammer. That's when I called the police and he left.'

'Are you sure it was a man from the flat below you?' asked the police.

'Yes! My neighbour even saw him leave, she can tell you.'

'Okay, we will go see him now.'

This young lady was scared to death and I can understand why. We took her to the hospital and she received stitches. The man from downstairs had left before the police arrived and they were still looking for him when we got an update at the hospital from a police officer— however, we did find out that this kind of behaviour was not unknown to the attacker.

Hopefully, he got arrested and sent to prison.

My second *nightmare neighbour* job was scary and particularly creepy. We got called to attend a 50-year-old male who had been assaulted in his home. It came down to us on the radio that the attacker had left the scene that police were due to attend, but they had no cars available at the moment. So, we got there first and had to be let into the block of flats by someone else that lived there due to the main buzzer system not working. I thanked the man for letting us in, however the guy didn't reply, he just stared at me. He continued to stare at me and my crewmate as we walked towards the stairs. I brushed it off as him just being a strange guy and carried on to my patient's address.

'Hello sir, my name is Emily and this is my crewmate ****, what's happened today?'

'Hello, thank you for coming. I was assaulted by the man that lives upstairs.'

'Oh right, I'm sorry to hear that. What did he do to you?'

'He punched me in the face and tried to force his way into my home, my wife and son are here! I forced the door shut and he was banging and shouting abuse through the door. Then he left.'

'Do you know this gentleman?' I asked as I was examining the swelling to his eye.

'He lives upstairs and he has been harassing my family for weeks. I have reported it to the police so many times. We are trying to get a restraining order. He waits for us to get home on the stairs and tries to attack me and my son.'

I'm going to add here that the son is about 10-years-old. My face at this point is completely full of horror as this gentleman continues his story.'

'He follows my son when he is walking home from school so now, I have to go pick him up as I am scared that he is going to do something to hurt him.'

'What on earth! That's awful,' I turn to the son, 'Are you okay?'

'I'm okay, I just want him to leave my family alone.' My heart nearly breaks.

'Why is he targeting your family, Sir, do you have any ideas?'

'Because we are not English, apparently we don't belong.' My horror turned to anger at this point and this was also the point when we heard this strange noise coming from outside the front door. I walked to the door and peered through the spy hole—all I could see was a figure walking back and forth past the door.

'That is him,' whispered our patient. 'This is what he does.' I described the man we encountered downstairs and it was the attacker. I then started to hear brushing against the door and that was enough for me—I quickly got on the radio and buzzed up for police and explained the situation.

Thankfully they arrived pretty quickly, but of course, the attacker was gone when the police arrived at the flat. They came in and our patient began telling them the full story of harassment his family had been receiving in the past few months. My crewmate and I hung back at this point, allowing the police officer to do their work while we were filling out forms for safeguarding. This is when the noise came back, that weird brushing sound. I crept up to the spy hole and realised the attacker was back!

'Hey, he's outside right now.' I whispered to the officers, who quickly sprang us and came to the door. Oh, the joy it gave me to see the surprise on this guy's face when the door opened and he was faced with two police officers. He was arrested on the spot and carried off to the police car.

We shared a cup of tea with the family before we left them to *finally* have a restful evening.

12

Miss, I Think You Should Take A Look!

I have worked many jobs with police officers now and these jobs are usually not of the nice kind, because the police have been called for a reason. Medical jobs that tend to involve the police can be violent ones for obvious reasons—often mental ill health is a cause— and the police are there for the protection of us and the patient depending on the extent of the mental health issues. For capacity issues, as we do not have the power to remove someone from their home against their will, except in cases where the patient has lost capacity due to a medical reason and we usually get the assistance of the police to help with this. Generally, these jobs can be quite chaotic and stressful and this job was no different.

We were called by the police to assist with a job at an overground station. A gentleman was reported to be shouting abusive and threatening speeches to people getting on and off the train. The police had initially gone to this patient and after talking with him they were suspecting that he was suffering from a mental health episode, so requested our assistance. My other female colleague of the day and I arrived on the scene and made our way up to the platform. When we got there the police had the patient restrained on the ground.

'Hello, what's happened here then?' I start.

'Hello guys, so the gentleman has been reported to us by members of the public stating he was making terror threats, such as bombing the train station. When we got here, he was very erratic and we couldn't hold a rational conversation with him. He then tried to lunge at one of my officers, hence his restraint on the ground. We would like your medical opinion that he isn't under the influence of drugs or alcohol so we can take him into custody.'

'Yeah, fair enough,' I crouched down and tried my best to have a rational conversation with the man but the officer was right, it was near impossible to have a conversation and his behaviour was indeed erratic. From these observations, we did get he didn't seem to be under the influence of any narcotics which could be affecting his behaviour. It did appear that the man was having a mental health crisis, and at least in custody he would be able to be seen by a specialist to help him.

At this point, the patient starting spitting at the officers restraining him so he quickly had a spit mask put over his head. (They are like a full-face fabric mask however they are see-through enough to still see the patient's face). Things began to escalate and the patient started to thrash about and fight with the officers. It was decided then that it was best to just get him off the platform as quickly as possible and into the police van. So carefully and with difficulty the officers managed to get him out of the train station. In order to do this, the patient was held completely off the ground by his legs and arms. We are now outside and just yards from the police van, I'm standing well back at this point, just staring on like a nosey bystander. This is when I hear one of the police officers scream out in pain.

'FUCKKKK!' The male officer then grabs his crotch and falls to one knee.

'Oh my god, are you okay?' I ask. I tried to walk up to him but he holds his hand out telling me to stay back. He is quite clearly in a lot of pain but soon he starts pacing up and down repeating: 'Fuck, shit, fuck.'

The patient is put into the van and the doors slammed shut as he hails more abuse at the officers.

"Are you okay? What happened?" my colleague tries this time.

'The fucker bit me. Can I go into the back of your ambulance and have a look please?'

'Yeah of course.' We unlock the truck and give him his privacy. We then work out that the patient would have had to bite through the face mask, the officer's work trouser and his underwear to reach his skin. That's one powerful bite. So, there's me thinking at this point the officer is probably just a little bruised and maybe also a little grossed out.

'Excuse me, he's asking if you can go in and take a look,' sniggered one of the other officers.

'You winding me up?' I laugh back.

'No I'm being serious he wants you to go have a look.'

I am not a prude, and in this job, I have seen many *private parts*, male and female. It is the nature of the job; however it is a rather strange situation to be in when asked to look at a police officer's private parts—because someone has bitten them! Anyway, I entered the truck along with my crewmate and we were greeted with the sight of the officer's trousers down and a torn testicle laying bare. The poor guy could barely look and I would be lying if I said the sight didn't make me flinch ever so slightly. I know the fuss men make if their testicles are knocked, so I could only imagine the pain this man was feeling, especially considering his testicle looked like it had been popped like a grape. So, we gave him a damp compress and reassuring smiles before we headed up to the hospital. Can I just make a point here that the patient not only bit through his face mask but also the officer's trousers and bit with enough force to cause a tear. Brutal.

I shouldn't laugh but this officer also found the funny side when we arrived at the hospital and we watched all the male doctors and nurses flinch and clench their legs when we handed over the story. Just like you male readers are probably doing now.

13

The Whistleblower

We quite often get calls from care homes for elderly patients. As you get older your body doesn't cope as well with medical conditions or they may have deteriorated with time. Quite often the elderly patient has many ongoing medical conditions and we have to figure out which one is affecting the patient at that moment. We also get called a lot for elderly fallers. Usually falling out of bed or chairs. But on this particular day at work, it was the first time I had been called to a care home by a whistle-blower for neglect of one of their residents. The job came down from police as a welfare concern for an elderly man in his 70s. The report stated his fingers were black with rot and his room was covered in mould and maggots. The gentleman's clothes were covered in urine and faeces. This report was quite alarming and of course, made us extremely upset. So, the lights and sirens went on and we started making our way to the care home. When we arrived, we decided to put our infection kit on just in case the room was as bad as reported. I didn't fancy maggots crawling around my boots and trousers. When we finally got all kitted up the police had arrived on the scene and we made our way in. As you can imagine the care staff looked at us in surprise and concern.

'Can we help you?' said one of the carers standing by the lobby.

'Yes please, we are here to see the gentleman in room seven.'

'Room seven? Mr Smith?'

'Yes please.'

'He is sitting in the lounge area, just through there.' The woman proceeded to point through the door to the right.

'OK, thank you.' The woman then scuttled off into her office.

'Mr Smith?' I asked as we all approached the gentleman. A strong stench radiated around him. His skin was dirty and his hands were black from grime and by the state of his clothes, I imagine there was some faecal matter on his hands also. His clothes quite clearly hadn't been cleaned in months and neither had he. Despite all this, the man looked up at us all and smiled.

'Hello,' said the man with a strong European accent.

'Hello Sir, my name is Emily. How are you today?'

'I'm good, thank you.'

'Good, erm sir, we have had a call from someone today who is quite concerned about you.' The patient is struggling to understand me at this point. Clearly, his understanding of English is basic.

'Sir, your hands are very dirty.' I point to his hands that are placed on the tabletop. He looks down at them, studies them briefly and shrugs his shoulders to suggest *they're okay.*

'Sir, do you want or need any help?'

'No, thank you.' I stand at this point and exchange glances with my colleagues in the hope that they know what else to do or ask. Everyone looks at each other just as stumped as the rest.

'Okay, Sir, can we have a look at your flat?' After a few hand gestures and using different phrases for the word 'flat,' the gentleman understands our request and begins showing us up to his flat. We all choose the stairs as the lift is too confined and I had to keep taking breaks from the gentleman's stench.

We reach his flat and the gentleman continues to smile as he walks us through his home. My jaw wanted to drop; however, my mind wouldn't allow my mouth to open. Every instinct told me to hold my breath for as long as I could. Every inch of carpet space was covered in rotten food, stains of a questionable nature, fag butts, dead bugs, food wrappers, letters, newspapers, clothes, and empty plastic bottles. This gentleman's home had probably not seen a vacuum or disinfectant since 1990. I have been to a few rather unsanitary homes now since my time with LAS but this is the first home I have been to where the carpet cracked under my boots. We had all seen enough and decided to discuss further—outside by the truck—for some fresh air. Myself, my crewmate and the police inhaled as if we were breaking the water's surface as we walked through the exit doors to the care home.

'What do we do now?' I ask slightly dumbfounded. The gentleman clearly needed some help but from our conversations with him it was clear he had the capacity to make his own decisions, and he actually wanted to live this way. Despite all our best intentions and suggestions to get help from the care staff within the facility, he declined, which he was fully entitled to do. Something still wasn't sitting right with me so I decided to call our clinical hub and discuss the case. We came to the conclusion that it would be in his best interest to send out his social team so they could evaluate his needs further.

It is safe to say the smell took a full 24 hours to leave my nose.

14

Well That's What You Get For Ignoring Me

At the peak of Covid, we were inundated with calls for difficulties in breathing, fevers, coughs, and general flu symptoms. So, when we got another call for fever and cough on a night shift, I didn't bat an eyelid.

We walked into a rather nice flat and were greeted by a woman in her 60s. She leads us to her bedroom where she proceeded to get back into bed and wrap herself up.

'What can we help with today?' my crewmate asks.

'I just don't feel right, I think I have Covid and I'm really worried.'

'Ok, we understand, well let's check you out.' I begin the checks, connecting this lady up to our machine, and read aloud the observations. They are all within normal ranges and medically she seems fine. Slight fever but nothing to worry about. So, from there, we recommend she drinks plenty of fluids, take paracetamol to keep her fever down and arrange for a Covid test to be sent to her house, and to remain isolated until receiving her results. If her symptoms were to worsen, she was to call her GP or 999 if it seemed like an emergency. Simple. Job done.

Let's jump forward an hour and we are sitting in the truck waiting for another call to come in. Only a few minutes pass until the truck alarm sounds and a job has appeared on our computer. A Cat 1. (Our highest priority) Cardiac arrest. CPR in progress. The blue lights are on and the truck is hurtling towards the coordinates given.

'What…' I hear my crewmate say as I'm navigating traffic.

'What?' I reply rather apprehensively.

'This is the same address as the job we just went to? It's the same age as our last patient as well, it can't be?!'

'No way! She was fine when we left her. Oh shit.' It is safe to say my anxiety was kicked into hyperdrive as we neared the property. Pulling up, we were met by another crew. We all geared up with the abundance of PPE and started making our way to the address. We were met at the front door by screams.

'Quick! Please hurry up she is not breathing!'

'OK, please stand back.' My crewmate says as we walk into the same bedroom we had just left this patient, no more than an hour before. Now I've mentioned before in my last book that you know when someone is big sick. This also works for when someone is dead. You quickly learn what death actually looks like and the difference between that and someone holding their breath. Or someone that is simply asleep. You may be thinking—well of course you can tell if someone is dead or not! Trust me, some people are very good at playing 'dead'. But anyway, I digress. We walked in and both quickly stopped in our tracks. Our patient was lying on the bed, quite clearly alive. My crewmate turns to the daughter who is looking at us in complete disbelief that we aren't saving her Mum's life.

'What's happened here then since we last left?' I ask at the same time as walking over to our patient and giving her a gentle shake.

'Wake up, come on, wake up. It's Emily, the paramedic from before.' No response. So, I try the eyelash test. This is a good one to see if someone is conscious or not. If their eyes are closed and you gently brush their eyelashes, a person's natural instinct is to flinch. And if they flinch, then it means they are awake. Or at least semi-with-it. Can you guess if our patient flinched or not?

Yes, she did.

'Darling, I know you can hear me. So can you open your eyes and tell us what's going on. Your daughter is scared to death and thinks you died. So please open your eyes. Because I know you can.' With that I see tears begin to roll down this woman's cheeks.

'What's wrong with her?!' barks the daughter.

'I'm not too sure, we were here about an hour ago and her observations were fine so I am not too sure what's going on now.' I then place all our patients back onto our machine and start taking vital signs again. They are still unchanged from before. The woman soon opens her eyes for a minute or so and glares straight at her daughter.

'Mum what the hell is going on?!' screamed the daughter.

'Well, that's what you get for ignoring me!' yelled back our patient.

'What?' I asked rather baffled at this point.

'You were faking it?!' shouted the daughter.

'You come round here and just talk to your Dad and ignore me! I have Covid and you still just don't care.' At this point, it's safe to say I started removing the equipment attached to our patient.

I quickly interjected before the daughter lunged over the bed to throttle her mum. 'Let me get this straight, you pretended to be dead to get attention for your daughter?' The woman quickly snapped her head around to me and replied.

'Don't speak to me like that you don't understand.'

'No, you're right I don't. But I think it's time we leave.' My crewmate and I spend the next few minutes making sure the daughter was OK and not permanently traumatised by this whole ordeal, but it turns out that the daughter is not surprised by the act and thanks us for our help, telling us she will deal with it from here.

Families aye!

15

Paramedic Humour

It's not all doom and gloom in this job, I promise. Where most of the humour lies in this job is with the other staff. You develop a dark sense of humour in this line of work. You need to, it's how we all function after seeing some of the stuff we have seen. And what's the point in going to work if you can't have a little giggle along the way.

I had started my 6:30am shift and the truck needed a service so off we went to the garage. With a cup of tea and a bit of breakfast, it was proving to be a nice relaxed morning. On the way to the garage, my crewmate started reading a post from the Facebook group 'Paramedic Humour' and not only did it make me laugh—it managed to sum up a paramedic's job and our twisted outlook on the role. We don't think we are heros, most of the time we are figuring things out as we go. And I'm pretty sure doctors and nurses feel the same way. Anyway, I liked the Facebook post so much I decided to tweak it a little, and write my own.

So here are my basics for being a paramedic—*The unofficial guide*:

- Truly sick people don't complain.
- The messier the truck, the sicker the patient, or the driver was a little too enthusiastic.
- When dealing with patients/supervisors/public, if it felt good to say then you probably shouldn't have said it.
- All bleeding stops . . . Eventually.
- All people will die eventually, just try not to be the cause.
- If the child is quiet, be scared.
- If the child screams, be relieved.
- Always follow the rules, but use your initiative to forget them sometimes.
- If there are multiple people unconscious in a room - DO NOT ENTER
- There will be problems.
- You can't cure stupid.
- If the patient sees the carry chair they will suddenly be unable to walk.
- Some things only a good autopsy will cure.
- If it's wet and sticky and not yours, LEAVE IT ALONE.
- Paramedics save lives, but it's the emergency care assistants that save paramedics.
- It doesn't matter what degree you've got—experience is everything.
- If the patient vomits, be sure to aim it at the bystanders that won't back up.
- If you don't have it, don't give up. Improvise, adapt, then call for BACKUP.
- If there are no drunks at an RTC (Road traffic collision) after midnight, then keep looking because someone is

missing.
- If it is stupid but it works, then it isn't stupid.
- The important things are always simple, but simple things can be hard.
- When it comes to needles, 'tis better to give than receive.
- Most of your patients are healthier than you.
- The address is never clearly marked.
- If the patient looks sick, then they are sick.
- Just because someone is fully immobilised doesn't mean they can't be violent.
- Don't underestimate the strength of a 90-year-old dementia patient.
- Always know when to get out.
- Always know how to get out. *Leave the bloody doors open.*
- Always answer the newbie's question, you were the newbie once.
- Always honour a threat.
- When responding to a call, remember your ambulance was built by the lowest bidder.
- You are not a Formula 1 driver, so don't act like one.
- Pain never killed anyone.
- All fevers fall to room temperature.
- Training is learning the rules, experience is learning the expectations.
- Be nice to your dispatcher; they decide which jobs you go to.
- The stereo must be louder than the sirens.
- There is no such thing as a textbook case.
- Mounted machine guns would work better than lights and sirens.
- Always expect someone to slam on their brakes in the

middle of the road when they see the lights and sirens.
- They said, 'Smile, things could be worse' so we smiled and things got worse.
- Always check the seat in a care home before sitting.
- Always check the floor in a care home before kneeling.
- If the family have moved the patient, be assured they will have been moved upstairs.
- All emergency calls will wait until you've begun to eat.
- When in doubt, remember the patient is sick and your ambulance has wheels… USE THEM!
- When referring a patient to a GP, make sure you tell the GP the patient's symptoms and don't let the patient do it. (A small cut could be described as a finger hanging off, if you get my drift)
- Patients will call despite only being on antibiotics since last night.
- You should stop CPR after the second 'OUCH.'
- You will flap on some jobs, it's okay.
- You will reach a breaking point, tell someone.
- And lastly, it's OK to talk and it's OK not to be OK.

16

Their Stories

I have made some great friends in this job, and some I have come to respect immensely as clinicians. When you begin this job, you realise that you will never stop learning in this profession. One of the best ways to learn is by learning from others. Seeing how other clinicians practise is a great way to critique your own practice. I figured at this point it was about time you heard from a friend and colleague on what this job means to them and how it has affected their life and their practice.

Mr W - Paramedic

My introduction to the prehospital world of paramedicine began in Australia whilst spending a year living remotely with my girlfriend (now wife) in a remote community in Western Australia. The town was so small that of the four emergency services, the Police were the only service manned by full time employees. The Fire service, SES (state emergency service) and the Ambulance service were all manned almost entirely by local volunteers. As newbies to the town and seeking to embed ourselves in the community, we signed up to all three.

A year on, having attended a variety of patients whilst on-call at night and working at a bank during the day, I moved back home to the east coast with a new drive and plan to become a paramedic.

Three years later, having completed all my University studies and placements, I began to apply to work for different ambulance services. Whilst several of the services were great, the London Ambulance Service (LAS) had caught my eye from the very first year of University. For the last seven years, the LAS had conducted a recruitment drive to Australia, seeking paramedics to join their Service. The application process, compared to other Australian ambulance services, was simple, and within eight weeks of applying, attending an assessment and interview day, I had a conditional offer of employment.

At the start of 2018, with my flights booked and my bags packed, I departed Sydney for London. Shortly after my arrival the acclimitisation to the British way began. Four weeks later, after a grueling month of death by PowerPoint and learning the LAS way, I arrived fresh faced and excited at my Operational Placement Centre (OPC) for 10 weeks of placements.

My mentor was a sharp, energetic and funny British lady with a propensity to avoid night shifts like the plague. How she managed it, I never knew, but across 10 weeks of placements, we only did three night shifts. I quickly regained my confidence in patient assessment and history taking, whilst learning new things like alternative care pathways, hospital handover processes, and the LAS way of doing things.

Look, I'm Waving to You....

One of my most memorable jobs during my OPC was attending a young guy who had been assaulted in an off-licence. As the bystander explained it, the patient was standing at the counter waiting to pay for something when the assailant entered the off-licence with knuckledusters brandished across his right hand. The assailant saw the patient, said something to him and then punched him hard to the head and chest, knocking him to the ground. The patient's foot had been caught under the counter and the quickness of attack led to his leg breaking in the process. Unperturbed by the pain, or maybe it was the adrenaline rushing through his veins, but the patient attempted to stand to defend himself when he was hit a second time from the other side, knocking him down again, and breaking his leg a second time (though this wasn't obvious to begin with).

As you could imagine, our swift arrival on scene was met by police swarming the off-licence and the howls of the man could be heard echoing down the street. On entering the business, the male patient was lying on the floor, screaming in pain, an obvious bony deformity to his lower right limb, and a sliver of bone exiting the skin near his shin. As a trio, we sprang into action, assessing the patient's vitals, administering Entonox for the pain, and attempting to get intravenous access to provide some stronger pain relief. We soon realized that the extent of the injury and our available pain relief would not be enough for this guy and an Advanced Paramedic Practitioner (APP) was requested. With 15mg of morphine on board (quite a lot) the APP arrived on scene and took our handover. He tried a few maneuvers to see if the patient's leg could be splinted to improve his comfort without much success. It was then decided that further pain relief plus ketamine (an anaesthetic drug used to sedate to reduce the patient's pain and dissociate them from the painful memory) would be administered to ease his pain and suffering enough to move him to the ambulance.

A short while later, with the patient high on a cocktail of drugs, we returned to the off-licence to find the patient talking and giggling to a packet of crisps on the shelf. When he saw us come in he picked up his injured leg, just below the knee and without any hesitation, or indication of pain, waved his severely broken leg in our direction, calling out in a mixture of laughter, 'Look, I'm waving to you'.

East London Paramedic Life.

The transition from OPC to my station group in central East London finally arrived and I hit the ground running with a mixture of enthusiasm and trepidation for what may come. For those familiar with London, being a Paramedic in the East came with its own varied blend of demographics, ethnic groups, hospitals, and the propensity to get pulled out of your area and sucked into the black hole of another.

As a Paramedic with LAS I worked in a variety of roles including on Double Crewed Ambulances (DCA) and Fast Responder Vehicles (FRV) responding to calls across a schedule of day and night shifts. I had the pleasure of working with an amazing group of people from all walks of life: from the UK, Australia, New Zealand, Denmark, the USA and Iceland.

In the eyes of the British public, the role of a Paramedic is one of a highly trained medical professional who responds on lights and sirens to critical patients 24/7, when the reality is usually much less exciting. We are regularly called to a range of calls which become a Paramedic's bread and butter, like abdominal pain, chest pain, musculoskeletal injuries, elderly falls, mental health, and difficulty with breathing.

While these calls can often come with their own quirks, over time they can become a little mundane. Then again, I'd happily go to them any day over attending a frequent flyer/high intensity user (a patient who calls the ambulance services more than three times per year—though for some patients we attend this number is more like three times per day). There is also a special place in hell reserved for people who call for the following (if you decide to chance us with these calls be warned, we won't be impressed): papercuts, hoax calls, your first time experiencing the flu at the age of 30, advice or requests to do anything non-medical (like calling us to change the batteries in your smoke alarm, fold your washing, or tuck you into bed), or anything that common sense would suggest does not belong with the word 'emergency'.

Fortunately, these times on the road, both as part of a crew and as a solo responder were also filled with some of the weirdest, funniest, vomit-inducing but also fulfilling jobs I have ever attended as a Paramedic.

Fall from Height.

It was mid-afternoon on a Saturday when my crewmate and I 'greened up' (became available) from a call we had non-conveyed, when a job came down that we were not expecting. A child had fallen from a height and landed in the middle of a busy road, approximately three miles away. I was driving for this job and floored the pedal, careering our ambulance towards the patient's location.

As we pulled into the location, I took in the scene: a tall residential building of approximately 12 stories with a large awning; below it a police car was already on scene and an officer was kneeling in the middle of the road besides a small object; on the sides of the roads people were gathering, phones out filming, and somewhere nearby I could hear a woman screaming. As we approached, the officer turned and we saw what we thought had been a doll, was in fact a male infant, no more than nine months old. The child was positioned on his back, wrapped in a onesie, and besides a small dribble of blood from his nose there were no other obvious injuries. The officer advised us that the child had fallen nine floors (~90 feet or 28m) from the flat above and hit the awning before landing in the middle of the road. We scooped the small child from the road and carried him to the ambulance where my crewmate and I could begin assessments. Moments later we breathed some relief when we discovered that his heart was beating strongly, and he had a good respiratory rate. Soon after the rest of the cavalry arrived, with HEMS, FRU's, a private ambulance crew and an IRO. Soon after, the child was stabilized, packaged and transferred on blue lights to the closest major trauma hospital for immediate treatment. It was later determined that despite a minor head injury, the infant would recover with no neurological deficits or life-changing injuries.

Death Certificate.

One rainy Thursday in January I was working a solo responder shift on the FRV when I was called category 1 to an unconscious 36-year-old male, possibly deceased. Due to my close proximity, I arrived within a few minutes and was hailed down by a family member outside the home. As I approached with all my gear, the family member informed me that I was there for her son, who had been lying in bed in the same position for several days and not moving. When I asked why they hadn't called an ambulance yesterday, they said they thought he was faking being sick and that he would get better. When they arrived to check on him today, he still had not moved and they presumed him dead, so had covered him with a bedsheet and called 999 for an ambulance to arrange a Death Certificate.

As I walked into the room, the first thing I noticed when I removed the sheet to inspect the patient was that he was both breathing, had a visible carotid pulse, and when I applied pain stimuli to his trapezius, he blinked. Now as a Paramedic I have seen my fair share of dead people, but I didn't need my spidey senses to know that this guy was very much alive, despite his family's impression and plans to certify his death. With a few more checks I quickly determined that the patient was suffering possibly the worst case of hypoglycaemia (low blood sugar) that I'd ever seen, that required immediate treatment and conveyance to hospital. Following some quick intravenous glucose and extrication to the arriving ambulance, the patient was blue lighted to the closest hospital for immediate treatment.

I Think I Made the Doctor Puke.

Whilst working on a DCA with my crewmate one shift, we were called to a 56-year-old male with an altered conscious state, vomiting and diarrhea. On arrival, we were met at the door by his carer, who advised us that the patient was a retired musician with a history of alcoholism, liver failure, drug use and depression. He told us that he visits him every second day and that we should prepare ourselves for the state and smells of his flat. He was not wrong; we needed the warning.

We were met at the door by a wall of stench—a mixture of alcohol, sweat, vomit and double incontinence lingered on the air that rushed from his flat into our olfactory centres. The patient was lying in a swamp of his own filth, his skin red raw from long periods in wet clothing, his long hair draped across the muck, and his eyes bloodshot and glazed over. A small dog was weaving in and out amongst the furniture, barking at us and the patient. After applying several additional layers of personal protective equipment, we waded into the scene to assess the patient. Our assessments determined that he was quite severely unwell with significant dehydration, a significant rash to most of his body, and a likely chest infection that required immediate transport to hospital.

Following a slow and difficult extrication and conveyance to the hospital, I relayed this story to the doctor during my handover. He too was gobsmacked at the state that some people let themselves get into when they don't look after themselves. It was then I told the Doctor of the last thing that I witnessed before departing the patient's flat. As we were preparing to leave, the carer was worried that the dog would not have enough food whilst his owner was in hospital. The carer grabbed a big bag of dry dog biscuits and proceeded to pour them onto the bed, on top of the patient's swamp of vomit, urine and faeces. The dog, who was clearly starving, leapt onto the bed and proceeded to chow down, biscuits and all.

As I finished telling this mesmerising tale to doctor, I heard a retching sound from one of the nearby sinks. Needless to say, I think I made the doctor puke.

17

She has stopped breathing ... right?

We as an ambulance service deal with panic attacks quite regularly. For those people that suffer from anxiety and panic attacks, it is a daunting and draining process. Your mind is telling you you cannot breathe yet that is the exact thing you need to do to overcome your panic attack. So, when we attend these jobs all we do is coach their breathing. In this particular job that is exactly what we did. A woman in her 60s called stating she was having a bad panic attack. We arrived to find her on all fours in her hallway, hyperventilating. She managed to explain to us that she suffers from panic attacks however this one was particularly bad, and she wasn't able to manage it with her normal breathing techniques. We assist her to her living room and sit her on the sofa. After a short time, she is finally breathing normally and feeling a lot better. I imagine at this point it was purely the psychological response of having us there that has done the trick as up to this point we really haven't done much. She goes on to explain to us that usually she blacks out and when she comes around she subsequently has a panic attack.

Now blacking out prior to a panic attack isn't normal so we carry out a few more examinations. She goes on to explain that her GP is aware and they have carried out many tests but nothing has come back with any answers. However, she does suffer from severe anxiety, so much so now that she cannot be alone with her grandchild as she is terrified something is going to go wrong. All of her vitals are coming back normal and there is no sign that something serious is happening to her (medically). We continue chatting and I'm asking her questions about her grandchildren and she is showing me pictures, it's all very relaxed and we are readying ourselves to leave this lady at home as she is feeling a lot better. Halfway through our conversation, however, she looks at me, panic in her eyes.

'It's happening again,' she says to me. I, at this point, think she means another panic attack is coming so I take her hand in mine and try to ease her mind, saying everything is fine and to just focus on her breathing. All of a sudden, her eyes roll back into her head and she slumps onto the sofa. I'm still holding her hand wondering what on earth is going on. This is when I noticed her face turn bright red like Rudolph's flipping nose. I quickly check the monitor and her vitals are still the same. She has in fact blacked out. I then turn back to the lady and my heart drops through my stomach and out of my a** as I notice she has stopped breathing. Completely in shock, I turn to my crewmate and say, 'Has... has she stopped breathing?!' After what felt like ages but really was probably no more than three seconds later I lean over her and check for a pulse. This is the precise moment my patient jolts out her arm and cracks me square across the jaw. I chomp down on my tongue and take a chunk out of each side. Trying to ignore the blood pooling in my mouth and watch in complete bafflement as my patient then goes into a tonic-clonic seizure. I might add at this moment that she has never been diagnosed with seizures—her medical records show no signs of seizure activity in the past. It lasts for roughly ten seconds and then she opens her eyes and begins to have her routine panic attack.

'Ah I'm having another one,' she murmurs. She has no idea that these 'blackouts' she is having moments before a panic attack are actually seizures. We get her in our carry chair and inform her that she needs to go to the hospital. Initially, she argues the point, saying this is normal for her she will be fine after a minute or two. Explaining to her that there was nothing normal about what she was experiencing and by the sounds of it she has been misdiagnosed for the last five years was difficult. I wasn't sure if it was actually a relief that came over her, that at least she finally knew what was happening to her, or horror that she has been having seizures all this time.

I would like to point out that if you do suffer from panic attacks, please don't start worrying that you are going to have a seizure, this was a very rare case and panic attacks do not bring on seizures.

I can only hope that with the right medication, this lady was able to resolve her symptoms and she can start living a normal life again!

18

Broken Nail

You may wonder what horrid scenes we walk into as paramedics. Well, this had to be one of the worst…

A 19-year-old had called 999 because she had broken her fingernail.

Yes, you have read that right. She broke her nail.

This is all.

19

The Past Can Come Back To Haunt You

I realised after I came back from my sick leave for PTSD and depression that some jobs were going to still affect me. I realised this pretty early on and I have been back on active duty for a year now, and still, paediatric jobs send my anxiety racing. I was recently called to a one-year-old that was experiencing difficulty in breathing and the parents described the child as floppy. Now the word 'floppy' is a big red flag for us. It means the child has lost all tone to their body. My mind will always flashback to that paediatric job that caused me to walk away from work for three months. The fear of being solely responsible for a child's life flashes in my mind and the realisation that when we walk in a parent is going to hand you their whole world and expect you to make it all better again. The responsibility is unmeasurable and rattles me to my core. On the way to this job, I remember my hands beginning to sweat, my normal anxiety response. My heart rate was on the rise and my mind was racing with all the possible outcomes that this job could bring. I have taught myself now to always expect the worse and hope for the best. It is the best way to not be caught out on a job and to ensure I thoroughly assess the patient before assuming everything is OK.

For some reason I felt the need to tell my crewmate that I was working with that day about my anxiety with paediatric jobs and about my previous experience. Subconsciously I must have thought it would help to know that my crewmate knew how scared I was. In a way, it did because he was extremely supportive and told me we were going to do this together and it would be OK.

We had trouble finding the property at first which only made matters more stressful because in these circumstances every minute counts.

Finally, we found the entrance to the block of flats and made our way in. The father greeted us at the door and showed us the way to his flat.

Mum was standing in the doorway with the baby in her arms. A very happy, smiley baby. Oh, the relief. It flooded me. You would think at this point my anxiety would fade away, but it doesn't work like that. My hands still shook and my breathing was still abnormally quick which I had to control in front of the parents. So, I plastered a big smile on my face and after a few laughs, we began assessing the patient. The parents were really apologetic for calling however the patient had vomited then suddenly stopped breathing, went blue and after a few backs slaps the baby began crying again. Of course, we told them to never apologise for worry about their child and to be honest what had happened sounded terrifying, so they were completely just for calling us out. I am sure all parents would have acted the same way. If you are concerned about your child and your gut is telling you to call an ambulance, then CALL

AN AMBULANCE. You will never be judged because children are weird and wonderful beings and no one knows the child better than the parent!

We took the patient to the hospital for a check-up and the moment we got back into the truck after handing them over to the nurses I finally let out a breath.

On to the next one.

20

Let's Talk About Mental Health

Mental health is getting talked about more and more nowadays, and that's really great. It used to be such a taboo subject and shameful to talk about it. This is fading with time but still crops up from time to time. Statistics show men are more likely to hide their mental health issues from others. The stigma of keeping quiet and carrying on is definitely more common in men.

Since being back at work I have been quite open about my mental health struggles and the reasons I had to take myself off the road. I no longer feel embarrassed or ashamed about it like I did at the time. I couldn't shake the feeling during my peak of depression that I was weak and needed to *'man up.' Everyone else is in the same boat as me and I just need to get on with work and not complain. Everyone has tough jobs and they don't let it affect them. I need to be stronger. I need to be better. Don't show weakness. Don't let them see I am struggling to cope. If my family know I'm struggling they will think I am failing at my job. A job I thought so hard to get.*

This is what depression and anxiety do to you. This is the

demon that is inside of your mind, controlling your emotions. I really thought for a time that I was the only one that felt this way and now I look back at that and think how silly that statement really is! I have spoken to a lot of colleagues now about this matter and every single one has 'that job' in their mind. The one that has stuck with them and crops up in their minds from time to time like a dark shadow on a rainy day. This is just my opinion but we as the emergency services are expected to keep calm and carry on, no matter the job. To be heroes, to be superhuman. To be battering rams of emotions and show no kinks in our armour. But let's not forget, we are not heroes, we are not superhuman—we are human. Shit hurts, shit makes us cry, shit makes us angry, shit makes us depressed, shit makes us sad. We are human.

I have spoken to police officers. I have spoken to firemen and firewoman and we all feel the same. We all suffer from stress and anxiety. It just presents in different forms. Nurses, doctors, carers, social workers, anyone working in healthcare can feel this way. Hell, anyone in *any* profession can feel this way. It's OK. It's normal. You are not weak, you are not failing, you are human. The best thing I ever did was start talking.

So, I beg of you, start talking.

Shortly after returning to duty after my time off, I felt another panic attack coming on. I was standing in my station waiting to green up (tell control we're ready). No part of me wanted to sit in the ambulance and head out to see the public, I wanted to get back in my car and drive home then and there. Work be damned. Now if you have read my previous book then you know my Mum is my rock, my support and my best friend. But by this point, I knew how worried she was about me and my mental health and I didn't want to burden her anymore with it. I decided to ring my Dad. My Dad is a very logical man, a very clever man, and very straight-talking. He is not the *'talk to him about my emotions'* kind of man and that's fine, I have my Mum for my emotional worries but today I felt like I needed to hear from him. I walked into our quiet room, (a place designed for emotional breakdowns to be done in private - yep we have them in ambulance stations) and I dialled the phone. He answered in his normal happy Dad tone.

'Hi Em.'

'Hi Dad' —crap I now don't know what to say or how to say this. My Dad has always seen me as a lot like him in certain ways: brave, working well under pressure, and can hold my own. And now I was about to tell him I'm literally crumbling at the seams. He is the last person I want to think of me as weak. Regardless, I break, I tell him how I am feeling and how I am scared to go back to work. I tell him of the very real fear that a part of me wants to get in my car and just leave and never come back.

What I get back from him I can easily say changed the course of my professional career. He told me that I hadn't failed anything. I have done what I set out to achieve. I had become a paramedic and got a job in the busiest services in the country... in the world. I had saved lives and if it was my time to throw in the towel, he would still be proud. He would always be proud. He also reminded me that I am only human and I can only do so much for people. All I could do was my best and that would be enough. After a few tears, I wiped my eyes, straightened out my uniform, and got back onto the truck and I still keep this philosophy with me each day. So, I guess this is a good time to say thank you, Dad. I'm still a paramedic today because of you.

21

"Please let me go to the party mummy"

Now you know what paediatric jobs do to me, well, try to imagine receiving a job down our screen stating that a 14-year-old girl was currently in a canal, unknown at this point was whether she was breathing or conscious. That job would be horrible, regardless of age, but the fact that it is a child just cuts a little deeper. The lights go on and we drive like a bat out of hell to get to the waterfront.

When we arrive, I see the police are by the bridge and two officers running over the bridge holding a defib and a first-aid bag. Oh yeah, adrenaline going now. We grab what kit we need and we begin to run over the bridge in the direction of the officers. But they're nowhere to be seen. We call out to bystanders asking which direction the police officers went and no one knows. Shit. We buzz up our control and no one knows where the patient is. This is bad.

Finally, I see a police officer running over to us waving his hands.

'She is out of the canal. She is over there with her friends.' Ah thank god! I say to myself. We start making our way over to the young girl and her friends, she is wrapped in a foil blanket. We finally get to her and it's freezing. She is shivering and as you can imagine we have gathered quite an audience. My crewmate asks if she wants to come to the truck to get some privacy and to warm up and she very politely replied, 'Nope don't need you, thank you.'

It wasn't the response I expected, but we continued:

'So, what's happened?'

'Nothing I'm fine. You can go.' her words slurring.

'Have you been drinking?'

'Yep.' She spoke so matter-of-factly.

'What's your name?'

'I'm not giving you my name,' she replies.

'Why not?' I ask.

'Because you don't need it.' The police officer leans over at this point and informs us of her name, which her friend has willingly given to the police.

'Why did you tell them my name!' she screams at her friend.

'Hold on, your friend has done the right thing. Someone has called because you were in the canal and you've been drinking. Something awful could have happened. We're not here to tell you off, we want to make sure you're OK.'

'Well, I'm okkkayyyy.' Picture Kevin, from Kevin and Perry and you've probably got the attitude down for this young lady.

'You can go now, byeeeee.' she continues.

'Did you fall in the water? I mean, what actually happened?'

'I don't need to tell you!'

Just breathe Emily, she is just a child.

'Look if you have to know, I went into the canal to wee.'

'You walked into a canal in *London* to urinate?'

Rolling her eyes

'Isn't that what I just said?!'

Okay, fast forward through the bizarre conversation as to why she chose to urinate in the canal and not behind a tree—like every other drunk person in a park. This is when things get complicated and rather infuriating. At this point, I would like to offer a huge apology to any teachers I gave any attitude to when I was a student. I experience this drunk, moody young female and honestly, it took more strength than I realised I was capable of, not telling her to shut the F-up. Please allow me to explain why—before you think I'm completely awful.

Duty of care is something we as clinicians need to stand by. It is the practice that we have committed ourselves to, to provide that person or persons with the care they deserve and/or need. For this young lady, we had a duty of care for her safety and wellbeing. She is underage, drunk, and not an hour before had decided to go waist-deep into a canal in the middle of winter. We cannot walk away and leave her to carry on drinking, just because she is telling us to *fuck off.* So, as she is unwilling to go to the hospital as a place of safety our other option is to get a parent to come and collect her and essentially take responsibility for me, so we no longer have to. With police on the scene, they have the powers to detain her for her own safety, (not under arrest).

When we told her this information it did not go down too well, she decided to walk off down the park, which obviously meant the police had to follow her around, which made the officers really uncomfortable. This went on for about 20 minutes, all the while the young girl screamed profanities at the police officers like 'paedophile' 'dirty pigs' 'molesters' and 'murderers' even came up at one point. This is when the officer decides to call for a female back up which meant another two police cars arrived on the scene. So, by this point, you have me and my colleague, four drunk 14-year-old girls, around 8 police officers, and a park full of people. Brilliant.

The police have finally managed to get hold of the patient's Mum and she was on her way to collect her daughter. This is when I and my colleague start receiving the abuse. I was a 'slag', my colleague was a 'dumb bitch' and there was more thrown in but to be honest, I stopped listening after a while. None of it bothered me or my colleague because they were kids. Not going to shed a tear over being called an 'ugly bitch' by a 14-year-old who had too many Bacardi Breezers.

My mind obviously went on to think of how my own Mum would react if she had received the call about her daughter being in this state. I would be lying if I said she never picked me up in a state or two when I was younger, but I would never have spoken to anyone the way this young woman was speaking to us. I know if I had done so, I would have got a clip around the ear—and rightly so. So, part of me was dreading the moment when the mother arrived because I knew I was going to be right in the middle of a family domestic, but let's face it, she needed a good telling off.

So fast forward around 20 minutes and the mother had arrived, she was clearly emotional finding the array of police cars and ambulances all there for her daughter. We informed her of what had happened and of course more tears proceeded. We reassured her that her daughter was OK, and that was what mattered most. The mother and daughter were reunited and this is when I thought the telling off would begin but it didn't…

What actually proceeded was the daughter shouting at her Mum telling her that she WAS still going to the party tonight and her Mum couldn't tell her she wasn't allowed to go. The mother buckled pretty much instantly and agreed that if the child came home and got changed and had something to eat then she would be allowed back out to go to the party tonight.

None of my business, none of my business. I repeated to myself as we got back to our truck and readied ourselves for the next call.

22

Time To Panic

'When I look scared, you can be scared.' This is what I say to patients sometimes when they are really worrying about their medical condition when really there isn't anything to worry about. It seems to give them some reassurance that everything is going to be OK.

Well, there have been times where I have been scared and I have failed to hide it on my face. This is usually when a patient is critically ill and I have no idea what's going on with them or how to help them.

I have said before that paramedics, doctors, nurses, and generally any healthcare providers are not walking encyclopaedias. We don't know *everything* and I certainly don't know everything. I have only just started my career and there are many things still for me to learn.

One of which is to try and remain calm when shit hits the fan. I learnt this when we were called to a woman's home in the middle of the night for breathing issues.

We arrived shortly after the call came in but couldn't gain access to the property. There was a key safe for the address but we didn't have the code. After a few phone calls back and forth, we managed to get the code and gain access to the property. This is where we found a woman in her 60s lying in bed. She was bed-bound, which is a sign that this woman had co-morbidities that are affecting her way of life, but at this point, this is all we know. Her breathing is extremely rapid and she is shaking uncontrollably. She is conscious and able to talk to us which tells me she isn't having a seizure; however, she is so short of breath she can barely manage a few words. Her oxygen levels are dangerously low and I fumble through the bag to get the oxygen out. She starts to claw at us as we are placing equipment on her, in her panicked state. I have no idea what's going on or why this woman is the way she is, but all I did know at that point is she was extremely ill and I was the most senior clinician on the scene, which bloody terrified me.

Do you remember one of my rules for being a paramedic? Your ambulance has wheels, use them! Well, this is what jolted through my mind as I stared down at this patient. My crewmate who had only been out on the road for a few weeks was desperately trying to attach equipment to this patient as that is our normal routine.

'Sod this,' I mumble to myself and run out of the house, I run to the back of the ambulance and grab the carry chair out of the back; racing back in I say:

'Don't worry about all that, let's get her out of here and go!'

Paramedics are meant to be cool calm and collected in emergencies and most of the time I am, but this particular night I was a fumbling mess. I'm not sure if it was her general appearance that freaked me out the most or the fact that I felt way over my head with this patient, but I was flapping. I began pulling the equipment off her and setting up the chair. My crewmate and I lifted this rather large lady out of her bed and onto a chair. The adrenaline really does give you a boost of strength you didn't know you had.

As I was so focused on getting this woman out of the house and onto the ambulance, I failed to notice that in all the chaos half of the wires from our equipment had managed to entangle themselves around the bed and the table next to it. So, when my crewmate started wheeling her out of the house half the furniture came along too.

Chaos.

As we got her onto the back, another ambulance pulled up behind us and it honestly felt like a gift from God because the relief was overwhelming. I was shaking uncontrollably and my heart was beating at 1000bpm. Moments later a team leader walked onto the back of the truck.

"Oh, we came to give you a hand but it looks like you've got this under control."

Under control! She is joking right! I'm about to have a nervous breakdown. This woman is pale, sweaty, in respiratory distress and there is a very high possibility that she is going to arrest on the way to the hospital.

'Can you stay for transport?' I plead more than ask.

The ambulance that turned up was part of the hazardous area response team so this team leader staying on the truck with me would have kept that specialist ambulance off the road and unable to help other people, but at that moment I didn't care. I need some support in case things got worse.

Which of course, it did.

Isn't that just the way, you beg the forces above to not let things get worse and that's exactly what happens, why is that?

Let me just remind you this woman had been shaking

violently since we arrived and I still don't know why. Shortly after we left the scene and are making our way to the hospital the patient stops responding. Her eyes become fixed and her jaw clenched. She is now having a seizure and still, I don't know why. The 'why' doesn't really matter at this point—what matters is we need to make the seizure stop. This is also the time that her blood pressure drops and we try desperately to get a line in but fail each time. At the beginning of our journey, we radioed through to the hospital to say we were bringing in a woman with severe breathing difficulties—now we are bringing in a woman with severe breathing difficulties having a full tonic-clonic seizure with no IV access. The hospital staff were a little taken back when we walked in all red-faced and flustered.

They worked on her for a while and it took around 30 minutes to stop her seizure with a concoction of medications. We had to leave and do another job before I could find out what happened to her or why she was as ill as she was.

What I did learn was when a job looks scary as hell, take a second, breathe, then freak out after the job is done. Ideally not during.

23

Your not wasting our time!

When we are feeling unwell we either go one of two ways; we complain the entire time and tell everyone that's willing to listen how rough we are feeling (this is me, not going to lie to you) or we stay silent and carry on, pretending it's not happening (my partner Chris.) Now, like I've said many times before, we as emergency ambulance crews are pretty good at guessing right off the bat if someone is rather poorly. It is in their speech, their breathing, their colour, and if I'm being really dramatic, it's in the expression on their face. For example, we were sent to a job which came down as a 65-year-old female waiting for a GP call back and for some reason 111 felt we needed to attend to this lady. So, of course, we did, we arrive at the property and the lady came down the stairs to open the door and we were waiting quite patiently, not overly worried about this woman. I mean why would we? She had stated she was just waiting for a GP to call her back so surely it can't be life-threatening, right? Well, when she finally opened the door, we were all rather shocked to see she was breathing at a rate of 40 breaths per minute, visibly shaking, and very pale. Instead of walking into her property as we normally do, we all effected a U-turn and took her straight to the ambulance without saying a word to one another.

She was in fact going through chemotherapy for brain cancer and was suffering from neutropenic sepsis. Good call 111.

Another example was one of the loveliest patients I've ever encountered. She was a 72-year-old female who had been feeling 'funny' for the last three days. Very short of breath when walking around and often felt dizzy. She had tried to get a GP appointment and finally got an appointment a few days later. However, before she could make it to her appointment her husband said 'enough's enough I'm calling an ambulance', despite the fact she was adamant she didn't need one. The husband also stated she had tried to get into the car so they could make their own way but she felt too dizzy standing up.

When we arrived, we could see how pale she was and how hard she was working to catch her breath. She could barely finish a sentence she was so short of breath. Straight away we connected her to the monitor and also carried out an ECG (Electrocardiogram). This is how we see the electrical activity in a person's heart. It's how we identify arrhythmias and heart attacks in the emergency setting. Straight away we could see from the reading that this lady was in a pattern of arrhythmia called Fast Atrial Fibrillation (AF). The is a condition where the two upper chambers of the heart receive chaotic electrical activity and cause the heart to beat irregularly and fast. A normal heart rate is around 60–100, fast AF can be anything from 100–175 bpm. This lady was sitting around 165, and according to her and her husband, she had been feeling these symptoms for three days! This is when I asked why she didn't call an ambulance when it started?

'I didn't want to bother anyone, I felt this before but it usually passes after a few hours,' she replied.

'Mrs X, you need to call us as soon as you feel these symptoms, your heart is beating too fast and this can be incredibly dangerous.'

'I'm sorry, I didn't want to be a bother.' Half of me wanted to pull my hair out and half wanted to hug her.

'You are never going to be a bother! If you call and it resolves then great and we will be happy about that but if you call and it doesn't resolve by the time we arrive we can help you. You shouldn't feel this way and it's something you need to be in hospital for.'

'OK, my husband can take me, because I know you're really busy.'

"We are always going to be busy; people will always get sick and need help just like you need our help right now. You're the only person we are taking care of right now. So, stop worrying about wasting time because you're not!'

Throughout the whole time we were transporting this woman to hospital on blue lights, as fast AF is a medical emergency that needs treating immediately at the hospital, she was apologising for causing so much fuss. Normally we are telling people that they're OK and to stop worrying, but there are some people that we need to convince they are actually sick and are in need of medical attention. 9/10 of these patients are from our elderly community. Stoic and hard as nails. When a family member tells me that their Dad or Mum or family member never complains—so now that they *are* complaining they know something is seriously wrong—I completely get what they mean, and trust that something is just not right.

I was asked once, after attending a job where a man called his daughter to let him know an ambulance had arrived to take him into hospital, how I would feel if I got that call. I told them I would freak the F out. My Dad would crawl to the hospital with a limb hanging off rather than call an ambulance, so if I knew he had called an ambulance, it's safe to say I'd panic.

I've said this before and I'll say it again: if your gut is telling you something is wrong but you also feel like you don't want to waste anyone's time, CALL AN AMBULANCE. Trust your gut and we can deal with it from there. We would rather tell you everything is fine rather than turning up too late.

24

You're gonna need to break the door down

On this particular day, I had the privilege of working with a fireman from the London Fire Brigade. Members of the LFB had joined the ambulance service to help us out during the busy Covid period. They were all amazing and deserve recognition for this!

So, it was our first job of the day and we were called to a 27-year-old male who was feeling unwell with a headache. We got dispatched and arrived shortly after the call was made. We knocked on the door but got no answer, knocked again and still nothing. This can happen so what we do is call our dispatchers and get them to call the patient back to see if they are in the property, and inform them we are outside. The dispatcher managed to get through to the patient who was still inside and he said he would come open the door but might be a while because he was struggling to move. So, we waited… and we waited… ten minutes have gone by and now I'm thinking what on earth is happening. It doesn't take ten minutes for a 27-year-old to get to the door even if they are unwell, so I call the dispatch again and ask them to do a call back to make sure the patient is all right. The patient answers and informs the dispatcher that he cannot make it to the door and we will need to break the door down. When this is relayed to us, I'm a little concerned and a little confused—-people don't usually want us to break their doors down as you can imagine. We as an ambulance service cannot break a door down unless we can visibly see the patient is in a life-threatening state, for example, we can see them bleeding out or choking through a window. You get my gist. Anyway, this patient was clearly breathing and alert according to the phone calls so we called for LFB to come along and pop the door open. These guys are brilliant at this, they have the skill to pop any door and leave literally no damage (most of the time). They arrived within minutes, so there I am standing outside this 27-year-old's door with about six firemen around me. I am a happily taken woman but the humour wasn't lost on me that this is probably 90% of my female friends' fantasy. Moving on swiftly...

They popped the door in about five seconds, which I'm not going to lie, was a bit of an anticlimax. I went up the stairs and found that there was another door to the property which was in fact the front door, which was wide open. The man was lying on the hallway floor standing at me.

'Hey, are you OK?' I asked.

'No, I'm not well.' I would like to add at this point he looked rather well which is always a reassurance. He had good colour and he wasn't struggling with his breathing, so at the moment these are all good signs.

'Why are you on the floor?'

'I can't move.' At this point, my LFB crewmate attached our equipment to the gentleman and all his vital signs were coming back normal. Another good sign. I was halfway through asking questions about what had happened today to try and get a sense of what was making him feel unwell when he decided to slump to the ground and for a few seconds flail his arms around before going unconscious. None of his vital signs had changed, and from experience, it didn't look like he was actually unconscious, so I did a few tests and nope—he was definitely still awake and alert, he had just decided to close his eyes and stop responding. This had happened to me a few times. Anyway, I carry on talking to him and ask why he is choosing not to respond. Still, I get nothing. We decide to try and get him up and lean him up against the wall. We assist him up but then he nearly knocks me flying as he uses all his force to keep himself on the ground. He is essentially fighting against us but still acting like he is unconscious. You know when you're trying to pick up a toddler and they throw themselves on the ground and fight against you? Well, this is what was happening so we just left him on the ground. It's where he wanted to be.

I was at a loss, he wouldn't talk to me and all his vitals were coming back normal but I couldn't just leave him lying on the hallway floor, so what do I do? Finally, I said to him, 'Do you just want to go to the hospital?' With this, the man opens his eyes, replies 'Yes,' then gets up and walks to his room to get his bag. I and my crewmate are still crouched in the hallway watching in disbelief.

After a conversation with his wife on the phone, it turns out she has left him recently and he is struggling to cope at home. He feels he need to go to the hospital so he can be looked after.

25

Sides of domestic abuse

If you have read my first book then you will know I have seen domestic abuse in my line of work. Some cases have been more subtle to notice and others have been blatantly staring me in the face. There are many things we can do to help, from providing victims with helplines and support teams, to rehoming and getting the police involved. A warning for those reading: if you have experienced domestic abuse or find this topic uncomfortable then I am giving you a heads up that I will be talking about emotional abuse and self-harm.

This one particular job came down as a suicide attempt by a 30-year-old male. He lived in a small block of flats and on this particular night, the patient's neighbour received a call from his girlfriend stating that the patient was trying to hang himself. The neighbour jumped into action and kicked the door down to find the patient with a rope around his neck. The other side was tied around the bedpost. The neighbour reported that the man was going blue and the rope was so tightly wrapped around his neck that it took some time to remove it from his neck. We arrived shortly after the rope had been removed and by this time, thankfully, the man was alert and talking to us.

We took a few moments to talk to the neighbour to find out all this information. We assessed the patient's injuries and his vital signs and they all seemed to be in normal ranges. With no lasting physical injuries, we decided to all sit down and start talking. Our patient didn't speak a word of English which made having a normally difficult conversation even harder, but with the technology of translation apps, we managed to start a conversation and began to piece together the events of the night, and how it ended in such a traumatic way.

The man began to open up to us about how his girlfriend had recently tried to leave him and how this wasn't his first suicide attempt. One week prior he had taken an overdose of his medications and spent the night in hospital. That was the night his girlfriend told him she no longer wanted to continue with the relationship. She had been with him when he had taken the overdose and she was the one that had to call the ambulance. The hospital had tried to refer him for mental health support but he informed us that he declined this, as he felt he no longer needed help because his girlfriend had decided to give the relationship another chance. This is when alarm bells started to ring in my head.

'Sir, where is your girlfriend now?' my crewmate asked.

'She is staying with a friend, she doesn't live here anymore.'

'Oh so are you no longer together?'

'No, she stayed with me for about a week then yesterday she told me she wanted to end the relationship again.'

'Is that why you tried to kill yourself again this evening?'

'Yes.' A moment of silence passed between us all. Mental health jobs can be so difficult as we are not trained, mental health clinicians. Clinicians that deal with a patient with mental health issues train for years in that specialist field. We as paramedics probably spend a month or two, combined, on the subject of mental health. The majority of what we learn about mental health is learned on the road once we are qualified. So, my worry here is that I am going to say something wrong or ask the wrong question and make things worse. I have witnessed the grief caused by suicide and I have even gone through my own depression but every individual that experiences some form of mental health problem is different and it's knowing *how* to go about their condition, with that individual, that can be difficult.

I have had patients that tend to open up more with the sensitive approach, or sometimes I have gotten the vibe that a more sensitive approach is best. Other times my patients have responded to a more direct approach. 'No bullshit—let's talk about your issues', kinda thing.

Like I said, each case is different.

Back to this gentleman in particular. We knew that considering the nature of what had just happened, we both felt that it wasn't safe for this gentleman to remain at home. We wanted to take him to the hospital as a place of safety and to speak to a specialist. Once we had explained this to him, he declined any of our help and stated he did not want to go to the hospital. This is where things became difficult. We always have to work in the patient's best interest and deliver the best care (as you have probably already guessed) so this patient's best interest would be to *not* leave him alone in the room where he just tried to kill himself. The best care for him would be to speak to a professional and try to work through what he is feeling—but if he declines that, where does that leave us?

We can only force someone to hospital if their capacity has

become impaired due to a medical reason. So, for example, if someone has drunk a litre of vodka and during the course of the evening fallen and busted their head open, we, under the Capacity Act can take that person to hospital essentially against their will with the understanding that they probably wouldn't be denying medical help and treatment if they did have the capacity to make a decision that wasn't impaired. i.e. the alcohol. Let's face it, we've all made a bad decision when we have been drinking too much. All 'capacity' means in a nutshell is that you can make a rational decision by weighing up pros and cons and coming to an effective decision. So, if you ask someone why their urine is black and their response is 'but Mummy, I don't want to go to bed,' (which has happened to me), then it's probably safe to say that person does not have the capacity to make a rational decision.

Now, I'm really trying not to bore you with the legalities of the job but I feel this job won't make a lot of sense if I don't explain these things. This is where we get onto mental health and assessing capacity. If someone is suffering from a mental health breakdown and while in their own home suddenly think there are demons coming out of the walls telling them to spread faecal matter all over the walls, (yes, also had this as well), and they decline our help, we cannot forcibly take them from their home and take them to hospital for treatment. Nope, we can only do this if they are a threat to themselves or to others. So, coming back to this gentleman, we could easily say he is a threat to himself. This is the second attempt to end his life and the reason behind it (his girlfriend leaving him) is still a factor—so who's to say that he isn't just going to try again once we leave?

We begin to explain our concerns about this to him and this is when the conversation takes a turn and his true intentions are revealed.

'I wasn't actually trying to kill myself,' he states.

'Well, what were you trying to do then?'

'I wanted to make my girlfriend feel bad for leaving me. I thought if she thinks I will kill myself without her then she won't leave me.'

———— (this is the sound of silence filling the room….)

'Sir, what about the overdose you took last week?'

'Yes, she told me she was leaving me so I decided to take them to get back at her.'

'But what if you had actually died?'

'Then that would have been her fault, and she would have to live with that. She told me she would give us another chance then she left me again last night so I called her tonight and made her listen while I tightened the rope around my neck.'

'What?'

'I did all this to make her feel bad, to get her back for breaking my heart. I don't want to die. It's all to get back at her.'

'That's… not OK.' (Professional I know, but I really am lost for words at this point.)

'Sir, you do realise that is emotional abuse. You can't behave this way. If you are really feeling suicidal then we can help but if this is all just to get attention from your ex and to guilt her into coming back to you then, that's toxic and domestic abuse!' His attitude throughout all of this was, *well this is her fault, not mine.*

At this point, I wanted to get a hold of the ex-girlfriend and see if she was all right. But she had stated to the neighbour she didn't wish to speak to anyone and to be left alone. I could respect that, and at least she was with a friend. So now we are stuck with a man that had a rope around his neck and, according to the neighbour, was turning blue when he found him, despite the patient's claims he was just doing this for attention. Do we leave him? Do we try to get him to the hospital? He has the capacity to make his decisions, but surely we shouldn't just leave?

In the end, we decide to call the on-duty mental health doctor and ask him to make a home visit. Due to the high-risk factor, we all agreed this was the best action to take, and surprisingly, the patient agreed to this. As you can imagine the mental health doctor that covers the northeast sector of London is a rather busy person so we had no choice but to wait for their arrival. Which took five hours. After one hour the patient decided that he was going to bed but allowed us to keep the front door open for access, but because we couldn't leave him, we had to sit in the hallway with his bedroom door open so we could watch him. I know, we are all heroes, right? Nope, I sat in a hallway on the floor for four hours watching a man sleep. It was approaching 6am when the doctor arrived and after a ten-minute conversation where he asked all the same questions we asked and got all the same responses informed us that he can stay at home and informed the patient to call 999 if he feels suicidal in the future.

So that was it, after all those hours and referrals we just had to walk away.

26

It's A Girl!

In this line of work, you will always have categories of jobs that come across almost like a checklist. It's like a list of jobs that you will experience as a paramedic—some people get them straight off the bat and others work for years without ever doing these kinds of jobs.

Here is a little example:

- Cardiac arrests
- Chokings
- Life-threatening anaphylaxis
- Life-threatening asthma
- Paediatric arrests
- Fatal road traffic accidents (RTA)
- Heart attacks (MI)
- Strokes (CVA or TIA)
- …and lastly but certainly not least—DELIVERING A BABY!

You can ask any paramedic and I would say a good 80% never

want to deliver a baby because if I'm perfectly honest it's bloody scary! It may be the most natural thing in the world but there are so many things that can go wrong. Midwives have to obtain a degree to do what they do, and that's for a good reason! You are dealing with two patients at all times and once that baby comes into the world, you now have to make sure they are both OK at such critical times in their lives—simultaneously. Mum can bleed out internally, baby can come out not breathing, or with the cord wrapped around the neck, the baby could even come out breach (which is my worst nightmare, this is when the baby comes out feet first). If that happens, we have around five minutes to get the baby out before they are completely starved of oxygen and go into respiratory arrest. Like I said, midwives study for three years at university to be able to do the amazing things they do, and doctors: seven years. Just to put this into perspective, in my training I had two lectures at university and one day at my induction with LAS on how to deliver a baby and how to deal with the complications that could arise.

So yes, it's terrifying. So, like losing your virginity for the first time, half of you wants to do it and see what it's like and the other half wants to run away screaming. (or… maybe that was just me?)

But the day came, and of course, it was the last job of the night. We're hitting about 5am and the call came in.

32-year-old Female: In Labour.

Now I have had this job come down many times before, when the women are in labour but hours away from delivery, so usually we call the midwives and they tell us if we need to bring them into the hospital or not. Well, for this job it was pretty simple what we needed to do.

We arrived at the address and gathered all the kit we might

need, which for maternity jobs is a lot. I don't know why this job gave me a funny feeling in my stomach but it's almost like I knew this wasn't going to be another case of materni-taxi. And boy, was I right! We walked into the flat and heard the cries of someone experiencing the worst pain in their life. The imminent Dad-to-be was pacing frantically between the hallway and the bathroom.

'Quick! quick, she is in here!' I immediately ran to the bathroom and was greeted by a woman lying on the bathroom floor with a baby's head crowning between her legs.

My internal monologue was going something like this - *Oh crap! Oh, shit, oh god, here we go, the baby's coming, OK remember your training, oh crap...w*hen actually my face was calm with a big smile spreading across it.

'OK, we got you OK, you can do this.' The Mum-to-be grabbed my hand and told me how happy she was that we were here. This is the point where I want to tell her I've never delivered a baby before and I was just as bloody scared as she was, but of course, I didn't. I squeezed her hand and then went back to the baby.

'Are you having a contraction?'

'No, one just finished.'

'OK, when the next one starts, I want you to push! You can do this!' My crewmate was with the Dad who was completely freaking out in the hallway; after a moment of calm he came back in and sat with his wife. Thankfully he was so distracted with coaching his wife he couldn't see the blood pouring out of her.

Not good.

Another contraction came and I told her to push and boy, did she. She had gone through this entire labour without pain relief and she was smashing it!

'Keep going! You're doing great, nearly there.' I have no clue what I'm saying but I know this is what they say on the telly, so I keep going with this.

The head is out, but I can also see the umbilical cord wrapped around the baby's neck; without even thinking I hook my finger around the cord and pull it over. I remove it a lot easier than I thought I would.

'One more push!' I brace my hands around the baby's head like I'm about to catch a bloody rugby ball, and out shoots the baby, along with an abundance of fluid. I managed to catch the baby and not drop....HER! It's a beautiful baby girl.

My crewmate quickly passes me blankets from our maternity pack and I begin to wipe the mucous from the baby's mouth. After a couple of wipes, I hear the most beautiful little cry. Her face flushes a crimson red and my relief nearly brings me to tears. I dry her off as much as I can and then place the baby on Mum's chest, skin to skin contact is so important moments after birth. It creates a bond that I can only see as something magical. Mum and Dad are in tears and my God I nearly am as well!

I and my partner are trying to fall pregnant so I'm fully on an emotional peak right now.

Now we have the waiting game of the placenta to be delivered. After around 20 minutes we begin to worry as there is no sign of the placenta, but Mum is starting to lose a lot of blood. The question now is do we wait a little longer or get going to the hospital? A ruptured placenta is a life-threatening condition and an undelivered placenta could result in surgery. We decide to make the move to the ambulance, I have the baby in my arms now while Dad gets the bags together and my crewmate is helping Mum get up and get dressed to go to the ambulance. All this time mum is bleeding quite heavily across the floor, out in the flat hallways and in the elevator. My heart starts to go a bit quicker when we get her into the lift and she goes ghostly pale. With one arm holding the baby and one arm holding Mum up, we get her to the ambulance and blue light her into hospital where she receives treatment.

What a way to finish the shift—we helped bring a new life into the world and Mum ended up being just fine! I ended up driving back to the station covered in blood and other bodily fluids but I couldn't be happier!

27

Please Drive Carefully, His Life Depends On It.

There is an expression called 'a sense of impending doom', this is where you have an overwhelming sense that you need immediate medical attention. Basically, you know you are about to die. Quite a daunting thought, isn't it? Well, I have never seen this happen to a patient and I am extremely thankful for this, but I have transported a patient that did experience this.

We were just finishing off a job at a hospital where we had to blue light this patient into resus, (resus is the part of the hospital for critically ill patients) when a nurse comes up to me and asks if we are free to do an immediate transfer to London heart hospital. 'Of course,' I said 'yes' and off I went to tell control that this is what we were now doing.

We came back into resus shortly after and were shown to our patient. A middle-aged man lay on the hospital bed. He had tubes coming out of his mouth and an untold number of wires and equipment attached to him. I asked them what was wrong with him and this is the story I got:

The gentleman brought himself to the main A&E and upon trying to check-in he told the receptionist that he was dying, and when asked what did he mean he started shouting, stating that his heart was tearing and that he needs help now!

I can only imagine what that receptionist thought. But it is safe to say that she got a doctor pretty quickly after he collapses in the A&E waiting room. He was rushed into resus where they found he had a dissecting aorta. Basically, his aorta that connects to his heart was tearing and he was bleeding internally. Blood was backing up into his heart and causing the chambers to collapse. He was dying and wouldn't last much longer.

The call was made and a specialist hospital in London was waiting for him to arrive. Now comes my part in all this. It was my job to drive a man with a heart that was literally tearing within his chest to this hospital.

We got him into the ambulance as smoothly as we could and just before I turned the key in the ignition, the doctor who was coming with us, leaned over and said to me, 'Please drive carefully, any bumps could put him into arrest.'

Basically, I have to drive through London on blue lights without jolting the five-tonne truck at all. Anyone that drives through London can appreciate how many bloody speed bumps there are, so now I'm sweating like mad. After a horrendous 20-minute drive, we made it to the hospital and rushed him up to surgery.

We managed to stay at the hospital for a short while to ask about his progress; the damage to his heart was quite extensive. They brought the man's temperature to hypothermia and that's how they performed the surgery in order to save organs and slow his heartbeat.

I wish I could tell you that the man survived the surgery and

PLEASE DRIVE CAREFULLY, HIS LIFE DEPENDS ON IT.

made a full recovery but unfortunately, he didn't.

28

Always Know How To Get Out Of Dodge.

One of my rules as a paramedic is: always know how to get out of dodge. Basically, always know how to get out of a place and leave pathways clear. This came to me so naturally when I started working in London, like it was built into my mindset from the off. Keep doors open and turn on the lights. You'd be surprised to know how many patients' houses we enter who are pretty insistent on shutting and locking doors after you've entered. And when I ask them to leave the doors open, they almost look shocked or offended.

Sometimes it doesn't always happen that way and sometimes you get stuck in a tiny hotel room with a man holding a knife. I mean what can I say, life's not perfect.

So, it was another normal day and another normal call, we were sent to a category three job which means non-urgent for a 25-year-old-male who was not feeling good. We arrived at the hotel and found out which room our patient was in. The manager escorts us up to the room, and before I get a chance to knock on the door, the manager has used his master key to open the room. Usually, we like to knock first, but the door was open now so I called into the room and I heard from the other side of the door the patient call us in. I walk in first and my crewmate follows behind. The room was so small that my crewmate only had space to stand behind me, she couldn't see the gentleman standing just around the corner with a giant kitchen knife in his hands. I must admit, at first glance I didn't see the knife because my eyes were drawn to the many lacerations that were covering his chest but it didn't take long until I did notice.

'Erm, can we open the door?' I ask rather hesitantly.

'What did you say mate?' my crewmate asks from behind me. This is also the point where the man just stares at me blankly, wide-eyed.

'Open the bloody door!' I start to push back and she scrambles to get to the door and literally, with no space to turn because of the giant O2 bags, I pretty much fall back out the door.

'What was that about?' she asks still none the wiser.

'He had a knife in his hand.'

'What! Oh, sod that, I'm not going back in there.' With that, the manager goes bursting into the room and walks straight up to the guy and grabs the knife out of his hand, and starts shouting at him for having a knife in the hotel room, which is against the rules.

I mean that wasn't really our main concern, but fair play to the manager for doing what he did.

I remember feeling so angry after that job was done, how I had ended up in such a potentially dangerous situation and had no idea at all before walking in. Sometimes jobs come down that sound dangerous and you can prepare yourself for them, like a stabbing or a drive-by shooting or even a road accident on a busy A road. At least you have time to mentally prepare for it, but when they just appear on you, you are left feeling afterwards nothing but anger and frustration because this isn't the crap we sign up for.

We shouldn't have to come into work each day and worry that one of us is going to be hit or kicked or sworn at, or spat at. We shouldn't feel that our lives are in danger or scared to be in the back of the ambulance with only our patients. I have been sworn at, grabbed, nearly thrown out of the back of the ambulance, had my life threatened, and at one point wrestled to the ground by a drugged guy that was trying to walk out onto a busy street. I have had guys try to touch me in a sexual manner, I have had guys try to kiss me. (Usually, they are drunk) I even had someone hit me with their car because I was standing in front of it trying to block the road so an ambulance could get down a single road to collect a critically ill patient. The gentleman behind the wheel continued to rev his engine and swear at me telling me to move, when I tried to explain an ambulance was coming (bearing in mind I am clearly in ambulance uniform) he then decided to drive the car and force me out of the way.

Just to highlight what I am talking about, here are some statistics from one of the NHS unions.

- In 2012/13 there were 14,433 reported attacks on ambulance workers in the UK.
- By 2016/17 the number of serious violent assaults on health workers had increased by 20% from 2012.
- 21% of ambulance workers have had to take sick leave due to violent assaults.
- 37% of ambulance workers have considered leaving their jobs due to the threat of violent attacks.

- 39% of ambulance staff have experience Post-Traumatic Stress Disorder.
- In 2016/17 81,669 days were taken as sick leave due to stress, anxiety, depression and related conditions in the ambulance service.

Of course, I'd like to sit here and say that one day this might never be an issue, but unfortunately, it always will. Some people are simply just not very nice, but others are influenced by drink and drugs, others are controlled by their mental illnesses. This is just the way of the world. Knowing this doesn't make it any easier though.

Sod the stab-proof vest, give me a taser.
   I'm joking, I'm joking.

29

Love Thy Neighbour

I always remember my sickest patient, they hold that place until the next job comes along and then I go, *oh no, you're my sickest patient*.

As you may have guessed, this patient I am about to talk about has become my sickest patient to date.

The only reason this man is still alive today was because his neighbour called the police stating he was concerned about him because he hadn't seen him in three days. Most neighbours go weeks without saying hello or discussing when the bins are being collected. But this neighbour decided to check on our patient and it was the best decision he could make.

The police arrived on the scene for a welfare check and when no one answered the door they decided to break the door down to check on the safety of the man living inside. They found the man unresponsive on the kitchen floor. At first glance they thought he was agonal breathing. Agonal breathing is essentially gasping, and it is not true breathing, but rather a brainstem reflex. The police officers believe this man was dead and drag him into the living room where there was more space in order to start resuscitation. I was told after the job was finished that when the police officers moved the man he started groaning and that was when they realised that he was alive. But barely. We got the call from the police and a message passed down that they believe he was going to arrest. For some reason, the job only came down as a Cat 2 so we were the only response being dispatched and we were only 0.8 miles away.

When we arrived, we grabbed all the equipment we could manage between the two of us and made our way up the three flights of stairs. Because of course there was no lift. I took one step into the flat and was hit with the smell of faeces and urine. The hallway was completely covered with rubbish and furniture. The flat was in a state of disarray and that is putting it lightly. I turned the corner into the living room and was met with a scene that will be hard to erase from my memory.

The elderly man laid on the floor amongst rubbish, dirt and grime. He was in only his boxer short and a t-shirt and I could see all his limbs from where I stood and each one was black. Not from dirt but from how hypoxic he was. He must have been lying on the floor at least three days in the state he was in for his limbs to be so starved of oxygen that they were basically dead. I could see the outline of his rib cage protruding beneath his t-shirt as he took shallow slow breaths. The entire left side of his face was swollen and turning purple right before my very eyes. There was vomit down his shirt and encrusted to his mouth and neck.

We all jumped quickly into action and the very first thing we did was place an O2 mask on his face. As I pulled the strap over his head, I felt my hand sink into something soft and squidgy. It was the patient's skull. From the very limited information, I could gather that he had probably been drunk (because of all the empty beer cans lying around) and had fallen back and hit his head in the kitchen. This is where he remained for three days. With his skull smashed in and a huge amount of swelling to the back of his head and the left side of his face. It was pretty safe to say he was bleeding internally around his brain. He had one of the most severe head injuries I have ever seen and his body was completely shut down. His heart rate was slow at 36bpm, his blood pressure was low, his oxygen levels never went above 60% on high flow oxygen and his heart tracing was weak. He was minutes from death. We had no time to waste, so between myself and my crew and the two police officers we got him downstairs and into the ambulance. We continued treatment on the way to hospital and as we started to leave, I put the defibrillator pads onto his chest expecting the worst. One of the police officers travelled with me in the back and it was extremely helpful. There was no time and a lot to do, so I began barking orders at the police officer which afterwards I apologised for, but of course, he told me no to worry about it. It all part of getting the job done.

I monitored his vital signs on the way to the hospital but they were just declining before my eyes. I kept trying to talk to the patient but he would just stare at me, almost like he was there still inside but couldn't speak. The swelling on the left side of his face was growing, probably because he was moved and it built the pressure inside his head. The swelling grew so much that his left eye was beginning to bulge from the socket. The flesh from his cheek was seeping out of his eye socket. He didn't improve despite our treatments but we did manage to get him into the hospital before he arrested.

He wasn't in the hospital long before he did in fact go into cardiac arrest and the hospital staff carried out a full resuscitation. He received seven shocks and was brought back to life and is now recovering in the ITU.

His thoughtful neighbour decided to make a call to the police that day and it saved the man's life.

After we had handed the patient over at the hospital, I went to the front desk to book him in and that was when the nurse in charge asked me if I was OK?

'I'm fine, why?'

'Because you're shaking?'

I looked down at my hands and released I was shaking and that's when the adrenaline crash began. I walked back to the ambulance and had to just sit there for 10 minutes before I could write any paperwork and process what had just happened.

Thirty minutes later we had finished the paperwork and were off to another job.

30

Life As We Know It

Oh, Covid-19, how you have just swooped into our lives and messed everything up. Well as I sit here, in May 2021, I can say with a held breath that you are on the way out. Shops are opening, restaurants are opening (kind of) supermarkets no longer have one-way systems that drove me crazy. Paracetamol is back on the shelves and the toilet roll is no longer stored in the cupboard under the stairs like Harry Potter. We are reaching a new normal. A normal still consisting of facemasks and hand sanitiser but more normal than 2020. Maybe I can look back at this book in ten years' time and say 'yes things finally did go back to normal' or maybe I'll say 'nope, things were never the same after 2020'. Either way, I am just glad our NHS can finally breathe again. Yes, we are still busy, we always will be. We treat sick humans and unfortunately, humans tend to get sick. But at least the word Covid is being said a lot less when discussing someone's medical history.

I think some people forget that this is not the only pandemic this world has ever faced. We survived The Black Death in 1346, we survived the American plagues during the 16th century, we survived the great plague (The Black Death's great comeback tour) in 1666.

We will get through this one and so will the NHS.

So, my final parting message is to the NHS workers. Imagine me waving that big rainbow flag. Thank you to all the health care workers that came out of retirement to help, thank you to all the nurses and doctors and health care assistants that got people back home. Thank you to all the cleaning staff that made the hospital safer to come to each day. Thank you to all the health care workers that lived in hotel rooms and healthcare accommodation because they had vulnerable people at home, just so they could continue to help those in the community. Thank you to all the carers that looked after the elderly when their family members could not. Thank you to all key workers that carried on during the lockdowns. You're amazing.

The world can be a scary place, but it's the world we have. So, take care of it, take care of others, and have a bloody good time because you only get one life and it is precious.

About the Author

My name is Emily L. Nash. I have been a paramedic for the London Ambulance service for three years and I love it more every day. I was born in Hackney, east London. I move out to the countryside as a young child and have loved it ever since. I am a country girl through and through. I decided to work for the London Ambulance service because in my opinion it is the best. There is so much diversity, so much culture and lets face it, alot more happens there. Why not start my career in the busiest ambulance service in the world. Yeah, thats right, you heard me, in the world!

You can connect with me on:
- https://www.facebook.com/emilynashbooks
- https://www.instagram.com/emilynashauthor

Also by Emily Nash

Just A Few Bumps
The tales and revelations of an office girl transitioning into a Paramedic. Tackling life with skills picked up along the way and enough Redbull to sink a battleship. The stories are real. The patients are real and the emotions are real.

My first book about life as a paramedic.

The Book Of Death

Paramedic Molly Black has spent her life wishing for more. Until one cold November morning, she is called to a patient standing on the edge of Blackfriars Bridge. With one giant leap of faith, her world changes instantly. Thrust into a world full of magic, Molly must figure out how to get back to her home with the help of Tobias. The man she met soon after falling into this new world.

Finding out that this unknown beautiful world is full of dangers and dark magic, Molly and Tobias set off to save the world of Elbonhelm from the evil sorceress Ada Gwyn. She must unlock the secrets of Elbonhelm to get back to those she loves.

Or will Elbonhelm and the magic it holds capture her heart along the way?

Printed in Great Britain
by Amazon